WELCOME

Ivan J Markov is an Australian-born architect and educator currently working in London. He undertook his academic studies at the Queensland University of Technology in Brisbane, School of The Built Environment, where he also completed his Graduate Diploma in Education.

THE HIDDEN TRUTH

a *Christ* dilemma

Ivan J Markov

Produced and Published by

Ivan J Markov

Independent Christian Worker◌

Ivan J Markov
86 Tanners Hill
SE8 4PN
London

Email: ivanmarkov@rock.com

First Published 2009

ISBN 978-0-9559868-0-2

Printed by: Lulu Press Inc.

Published by the Author

Cover photo titled 'A Scottish field' by Evica Tominovic © 2009, Zagreb,
Republic of Croatia. Used with written permission.

Dedication

This book is dedicated to all the children of the earth.

Acknowledgements

To acknowledge firstly the 'family' at Journey's, Greenwich which provided me shelter and a home away from home while I toiled on this project. A special thanks to Yvonne, Vern and Janet who watched over me like mother hens. I would also like to thank all the many people who believe in my work and encouraged me when at times I felt like giving up, bless you all.

Many thanks to Krzysztof Krajewski (Max) for introducing me to the idea of self publishing on-line and providing me with some great tips.

The bible used in all referencing in this book is the 'Pocket Companion Bible' New King James Version, published by Thomson Nelson Publishers in 1991.

All concordance and cross-checking was conducted using an online bible and search engine called Bible Pro from BibleOcean.com, version: 12.16.0.0.

TABLE OF CONTENTS

Introduction

I want to begin this special book with a genuine prayer to God, the creator of this world. When I say world I do not speak of the world created by man's hand or his devices but the miracle and true glory of creation. Snow topped mountainous peaks, wild flowing rivers, tree lined creeks, the animal and plant kingdoms in their entire splendour.

Father my God and my true friend I humbly ask you now for your help and guiding hand. I am here as your servant and I pray your trusted scribe. I empty myself into your loving hands and sincerely ask you to help me as I am small before you and am not fit to be associated with your name or kingdom. I feel I am unworthy but I will not allow these feelings to become an excuse not to serve you. I realise that there are no secrets or hidden places from your eyes. You look deep within all our hearts not for the intention of harm but for the purpose of Love and Mercy. Please help me to write this book, help me to empty myself before you so that the truths which you want the world to know can be written. I know many of your words have been spoken and recorded in the books of the bible and other inspired texts. Please bless and help me now to diligently and honestly compile the chapters of this– your book.

This is written for the world as a truthful guide and a continued testament for the peoples of the earth who genuinely want to know about why we are on this planet. At times it appears that we are comfortable at home and we have no need to seek a life beyond our earthly confines. As we grow older, we taste the cruel reality of our fragile human existence with all its weaknesses and failings.

Of all ideals that one can pursue on this earth, truth is of all the most difficult to completely grasp. The problem with truth is it's like looking at a grain of sand. With the naked eye it can be recognised as a tiny stone. But through a lens or microscope its appearance changes into another world with spectacular shades of colour and undulating textures. It is the same with truth, it can have many dimensions and windows.

In the end there can be only be one truth; but one needs the special eyes to see. What we really face here on earth is not so much to find total truth but rather to make a choice. We are called to either accept the eye witness and testimonies of spiritual authorities' such as the apostles John and Paul or to call them and all the prophets including Jesus liars.

Jesus, yes a prophet and miracle worker but God himself in the form of man and a son, who openly stated: 'Before Abraham was, I am' (John 8:58). Who visited our earth in the likeness of a human being for a short time. Before his hurried exist, hinted that he had many more things he wanted to tell; that he would send us a teacher, a helper being the Holy Spirit, who would lead the children of God unto all truth. So we are really blessed now in this world to have such a helper and it is with this helper who I call the 'quiet achiever' that I write this book, a warm and loving presence. I humbly pray it will help especially the young children of the earth who mostly are born into a brutal and cruel world with their pockets already emptied. Rich blessings such as access to natural resources, stolen and hidden away, intended by God as a free and natural birth right for all the earth.

In our modern world of today it appears we have multiplicity of choice and a wide variety of options. It is easy to literally become lost in an endless array of idealistic pursuits such as technology, sport, high finance, astrology or ancient mystic philosophy. I wonder can there really be any area more important than establishing a genuine link with our creator not to mention the question of: The eternal destination of our soul?

To some people God is acknowledged and in many cases accepted as an intelligent overseeing entity; somehow detached yet responsible for the world we live in. To others God is something to disprove and also dishonour as they feverishly search, looking for reasons and opportunities to disprove his existence, in turn justifying their own state of unbelief.

As a youngster when I started my own journey of truth I often became frustrated almost to the point of tears wondering, what is the human race trying to prove? How can people not believe in God or the simple words of Jesus his son? I noticed just at the mere mentioning of his name a reaction. To some it caused immediate silence, to others it seemed to be a call to a lunging desperate rage. The behaviour seemed exactly the same as the masses displayed at the time of Jesus' murdering just over two-thousand years ago.

Jesus, this most beautiful man came gently to 'those who had ears to listen' telling stories with hidden secrets and messages for his people first then to the entire world. To some he appeared rigid fighting against injustice and especially hypocrisy and lies. For others he performed wonderful miracles of healing, was preyed upon, betrayed, then abandoned and finally slaughtered. Even at his killing he was rejected by heaven itself and was lowered into the bowels of the earth where he dwelt among the ancient lost souls long forgotten but still somehow existing deserving a mention in the New Testament writings. By God's power or who knows? Even his own, ascended first out of the earth and rose again first to its surface then after a time ascended up into heaven itself to sit at the right hand of God and continues with his special work in the inner tabernacle behind the veil even to this very day.

My question is why are some people still angry? Is it because they sense within themselves that he isn't actually dead even though he was killed? That the human race has exercised its penultimate weapon of murder to extinguish this fire which was started; but it could not. The name *Jesus* despite its continued abuse and youthful mockery continues to be a name above all the names of the earth. A continuing conundrum, to some a dilemma, to others deep thought and contemplation; but always able to generate discussion and debate.

When I read in the book of Genesis about the serpent, Lucifer directly questioning Gods words and murmuring behind his back I realised here lay the root to the great dilemma of truth. Only

Lucifer and his spiritual children have the audacity to question God's word and talk out of place before our creator. Being born at the end of this age it is sometimes easy to forget that this early seed of disobedience has grown over many thousands of years into a gigantic monster with great powers of blasphemy and unspeakable abominations.

This book is based upon an acceptance of God as originally revealed to a nomadic people, a Jewish tribe led by Abraham who genealogically can be traced back to the first spiritual family of the earth, Adam and Eve. I do not want the reader to be discouraged if they do not understand the entirety of what I am saying. Truth is something which is hard to be ignored as it seems naturally to rise up to a surface where it can be viewed and considered. All inspired books are filled cover to cover with truths. To ignore early or late Testament writings as nothing would be straight out thoughtless and foolish, especially in a book like this.

It is with the help of this same God as described in those sacred books that I am here now writing. I dare not to be alone but am relying on them to guide me, bless, and go on to help you, the reader, understand and re-open age old mysteries which are revealed herein.

Authors Note

This book is not a scientific treatise but a spiritual philosophical book and should be read with this in mind. I am not here to labour or try to prove that God exists; every person must make this very crucial decision on his or her own. What I can say is this: it has been written with the most sincere and deepest love from a simple man who feels it only right and honest to leave a legacy of my knowledge and explanations of discovered truths and experiences which are taking place on this earth today.

The chapters and topics covered will not be easy to absorb and at times challenging to understand. To a few my words will be like water to a thirsty plant. To others my ideas will be offensive to the point where some will harbor thoughts of murderous rage. So please don't take what I write personally as in the end it is only a book and every person in a free and democratic world has a basic right to express his or her opinion without fearing persecution.

What I can tell you is as you work your way through each chapter you have the answers to many ancient questions which not many people have the honesty or courage to write about today. As I already stated in my *Introduction*, truth is a very difficult notion, and often the best we can have is a feeling about it. I do hope to discover more detail and truths myself as my own journey continues.

I never want my words here to overshadow the words of Jesus and his holy prophets. Let what I write always be counted last behind the least of them all.

The biggest problem or obstacle the world today has is Jesus. In the Muslim world he is regarded as nothing more than a simple prophet. To the Christian world he remains a serious dilemma. He proclaimed to be 'the way, the truth, and the life' (John 14:6) and no one can come to the Father or even into heaven itself but 'through him'. This is a big claim and with these few spoken words, and of course others, Jesus purposely placed himself above all mankind, every prophet, every hidden hope, anything created, past, present and future on earth and the universe itself.

To those who believe in these words even blindly, find hope, direction and peace. Those who are frauds are very quickly 'found out' and are directed towards their true hearts desire which is sin and corruption. One thing Jesus clearly came to stop was ignorant sin. For the true Christian and follower of Jesus Christ; the resisting of sin must be a major priority, otherwise, what ever journey you think you are on is simply a futile waste of time.

Reading the sixty-six books of what man compiled and called "The Bible" is not essential in knowing God; but for someone wanting to know him better, reading and meditating on at least some of the words written would be a natural and sincere progression. If you truly love somebody you would desire to read their actual words and try to get to know that person with all the energy and might you possess. If you do not then you are simply kidding yourself and God.

I have resisted quoting passages of scriptures and then offering interpretations that have the potential to misguide and distort. This seems to be a standard recipe used by religious fundamentalists and other superstars of God in both preaching styles and written material. To help ease my conscience scriptures are quoted sparingly to commonly known practices or sayings of Jesus and the prophets. I have also included some 'key', not so well known, references that need to be uncovered which have become lost and forgotten over the passage of time.

This is a book not written for profit, personal glory or gain but for love and edification. I struggled over many years to compile and present this book. Personally I hate even compilations such as this work which could possibly overshadow the word of God as spoken by Jesus and the prophets. Yet I have noticed as the years trickle by the essence of truth has become increasingly clouded. Sadly this is a perpetual state in which the human race enjoys finding itself. Always crying out in its suffering and misery just as the lepers called out for help in their torment as Jesus walked near.

Please enjoy reading this book. May it be a comfort and a light to you, helping to unlock answers to key questions of this world; the greatest being our own fallen spiritual state. I am pleased that God has brought this book to you at great personal cost, I wish you all the peace, happiness and prosperity which is promised with the gospel message and to those who understand his learned ways.

Part One

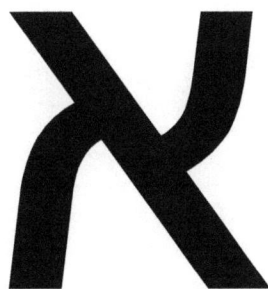

1

To Believe or not to Believe

When Shakespeare wrote the words: "to be, or not to be, that is the question" I wonder was this great playwright and poet just another thief, one of many in this world who have stolen images and sayings from the sacred Jewish texts. Diluting, twisting inspired words and ideas, plagiarising and then claiming fraudulently the rewards intended for others who serve God and humanity honestly and creatively, yet received no remuneration or acknowledgment, rather insults mockery and humiliation, and in the end a cruel and silent death.

To believe or not to believe is clearly an image from the bible and correctly acknowledged as such. Unbelief is very much part of our human condition and a regular theme in all dialogue and discussions about Jesus today and in times past. Belief in Jesus, as recorded in the New Testament accounts, was always a dilemma. Belief was a problem, which even the closest disciples of Jesus struggled, as seen with Peter and of course Thomas. To believe or "to be" indeed brings with it a "sea of troubles" (Shakespeare) and sometimes it's safer and far easier to simply not believe.

The most powerful image of this dilemma of belief is seen with the two other men crucified with Jesus. According to our special human eye witness, John, there were two other men crucified on either side of Jesus. The supposed dialogue is recorded in Luke, although not an eye witness account, it carries a telling image of one who believed and the other who did not.

So what to say about the one who believes and the one who does not? One thing every person has is the right to one's own belief. There is no doubt many in this world exercise this belief and rightly so. In the end who really has the right to ever force another human being to do anything? Accept of course our creator.

Unbelief is actually part of our human condition and a normal part of being human. As written in the book of Genesis, at the beginning just after the creation of the universe and the earth, mankind was eternally separated from God. From this time two worlds existed one where God dwelt and the other this earth. Although, once connected through Eden and 'the garden', since 'the Fall' this world now exists almost totally independently and is in fact fuelled only by the original power of this once, and still, magnificent creation. Being separated from God for so long it is actually a natural and honest thing to carry within ourselves unbelief.

When the world was separated by vast and dangerous seas believing it to be flat was widely accepted. Because of this isolation nations and tribes of the earth most definitely grew and developed independently as worlds within a world. What was believed and practiced was only what that independent world or people were actually experiencing.

It is a fact that we are separated from God. There is no doubt that both worlds exist independently from each other just as the 'old worlds' used to. Jesus gave hints of these separate domains in the gospel writings: 'My father gives you true bread from heaven. For the bread of God is He [Jesus] who comes down from heaven and gives life unto the world' (John 6:32-33); 'You are from beneath; I am from above. You are of this world; I am not of this world' (John 8:23); and 'I have other sheep not of this fold' (John 10:16).

While the world has obviously changed, and sadly continues to do so, this planet was never designed for the purpose of total unification. It is written many times in the Old Testament: 'every man to their tents' (II Kings 14:12) whether that tent is made of ice, camel skin, stone, brick or straw. What is implied here is that a household or tent should be as private and secure as what the tent itself is suppose to represent.

It's funny as there actually is more honesty in a person or household that says they don't believe than a person who simply pretends to believe. The problem with many years of pretending or lying [to believe] one eventually falls into the natural progression or state of unbelief; often with diabolical and irreversible consequences.

This world, actually this planet is not with God, it is in the process of being destroyed. A clear consequence of sin and as it is written, 'For the wages of sin is death' (Rom. 6:23). Our human ancestors chose to eat from the tree of knowledge of good and evil and it is also written: 'you shall surely die' (Gen. 2:17). If we do not believe and accept this original consequence made by God then we still stand together as one with the serpent in rebellion which in essence is actually the most pure form of unbelief.

So as [we] the world, in majority, continue in rebellion and unbelief to not believe is actually the most honest state that we can find ourselves to be before God. Early in Peter's calling he had belief and reverence for Christ. This is seen when he threw himself at Jesus' feet begging him to: 'depart from me as I am a sinful man, Oh Lord' (Luke 5:8). To accept one's own sinfulness is the most honest reaction that one can have when exposed to such a sinless and holy person.

Unbelief is acceptable to God and his love extends well past its boundaries as many a hard hearted person has already discovered. Some of them when converted, sadly, love to then dramatise their own conversion as if they are some big win or trophy for Gods kingdom. Unbelief was something that Jesus himself marvelled at. With so many things around to remind us of the goodness and presence God, such as nature, how can unbelief and faithfulness co-exist?

The real problem is when unbelief moves into the next stage; one of denial. Interestingly Peter the one who was first to recognise Jesus as the Christ and honour him also suffered from a serious problem of denial. I suggest that it was more cowardice rather than the pure form of denial. No doubt this hurt Peter more than I think Jesus; but after asking Peter at the fish breakfast, three times 'Do you Love me?' (John 21:16), I think was enough punishment for a poor man plagued with so many problems which I am sure continued well until the end of his life. Jesus also spoke about denial declaring that: '... whosoever shall deny me before men, him will I also deny before my Father which is in heaven' (Matt. 10:33).

The reason why denial is so serious is it is actually a form of mockery of whom and what Jesus is all about. To deny a most pure gift that can be given from the heart of heaven not just an image like us but the actual Son is to deny something which is beyond criticism or enquiry. It is declared also in the scriptures that, 'Today, if you will hear His voice' (Heb. 3:7). This is the day and occasion of one's salvation, there is actually no tomorrow. The very first moment one hears of the message of the gospel is the exact moment a dye is set for one's own personal salvation. It doesn't matter what course life will take or even to what religion you belong it will always return to the first moment when you heard that God had sent his only Son to this earth to show us 'the way, the truth and life' back to God. True belief is actually the earliest beginnings of a very special process called reconciliation.

Some people in this world are deluded with the belief that somehow a person called Jesus came around two-thousand years ago and miraculously fixed something that was broken and now its 'party time', no need to worry let's just ride the bus to paradise.

The New Testament writings clearly illustrate that our first obligation and duty is to reconcile with God. To reconcile with someone is not simply to say the empty word "sorry!" The word sorry on its own in reality is a form of mockery further compounding the injury as in actuality sorry is "too late!" Because the damage is already done, continuing to be damaged. Something is still broken until it is repaired. Unless something is restored back to its original state it is still broken. What is really in order is reparation and replacement or at the very least reconciliation with alternative arrangements set in place with the injured party.

If we, like Adam, begin to search around for excuses and say "well it wasn't me that picked and ate from the plate of disobedience," well we are like our spiritual ancestor, continuing and also suffering the same curse and judgement. Belief and interestingly even unbelief, to a degree as stated earlier, is actually the beginning of what is a genuine chance for our own reconciliation with God himself.

The old and new testament clearly record many people who have gone to great lengths to reconcile with God. The greatest man that walked on the earth is of course Jesus. The greatest man born from the seed of a woman is John 'the Baptist' and Jesus spoke of this fact and added that even the smallest in Gods kingdom was greater than He; but of course we human beings don't like this do we? Again we turn to our old faithful friend 'unbelief' shielded with denial which has served us so well from the very beginning.

It was well known at the time of Jesus, actually just before, even to this very day that a special man called John the Baptist called people from everywhere to put a stop to the old ways of lying, cheating and deceiving one another. Johns' whole purpose was to 'prepare the way of the Lord' calling everybody to repent and be baptised. In this way you are showing God, who sees all things from heaven, through the humbling of public baptism that you personally are stopping what you can and beginning the process of reconciliation or making up with God.

Remember this, that we are not ever fully reconciled with God until we are again walking with him in the cool of the evening in his garden and we can again be called God's friend, like Adam and Moses, face to face.

It's easy to be a friend to someone who has good things for you but what about becoming a friend with someone who is killing and destroying your body and soul as the Father is doing as a consequence for sin to the vast majority of all mankind.

The Baptist stated: 'an axe is laid at the root of every tree' (Matt. 3:10). Jesus extended on this to say: 'Every tree that brings forth not good fruit is hewn [cut] down, and thrown into the fire' (Matt. 7:19). It's easy to say we are friends with Jesus' a simple son who came [largely] as an ally, healing the sick, blessing children, guiding and feeding the hungry; but to be friends with the Father again with a pure and mutual trust? This is a completely separate matter set aside for the deepest contemplation.

On the issue of reconciliation the page stops with Jesus the only human being to be reconciled with the Father and in the end taken up into the clouds escaping the clutches of corruption and death.

Jesus as a young boy was well versed in the scriptures. This is a clear example that he loved the words of his father in heaven spoken through the prophets. It could be argued that he was forced to read these scriptures like most religious children; but his time in the temple with the elders demonstrated the purity of his passion, a natural and unforced relationship with his heavenly Father.

It may seem strange for you to read that Jesus from the moment he was placed inside his mother's womb was faced with the same burden of reconciliation as human children of the earth are faced with today. Taken from the sanctity of heaven and placed on the earth as a fragile, vulnerable infant. The simple fact that he was a human being made him already part of our human condition subject to universal [earth] condemnation, sin and death.

2

Salvation is of the Jews

The ten commandments of God were written twice by Gods own fingers and given to the Jewish people for safe keeping, the people whom God chose personally out of all the tribes of the Earth. This was later taken from them yet it was never intended for the world as a whole but for one special tribe of people. It is well known and even expressed by Jesus himself, that, 'salvation is of the Jews' (John 4:22). Jesus was born a Jew and really for all intensive purposes is still a Jew. What I am trying to get to here is that the civilised world especially the empires of the ancient and modern world such as the Roman and British empires adopted and used the Ten Commandments as if they were given to them also by God; but these sacred words treasured and revered by the Jewish people were never meant to be in the hands of the Gentiles or non-Jewish people. Most certainly, they were never meant to be used to manipulate and justify nations, to commit injustices or to commit a multitude of wrongs around the world.

Many countries and nations in our world would look pretty empty; actually, naked without having many of these misappropriated words and images lifted from the original sacred Jewish texts and embedded into their own constitutions. My question here is, who or what person has the right to use these words of God given to one tribe, one people, and enjoy the truthful powers that it possesses?

There is no doubt that having these sacred scriptures available to the world to read can help us to understand more intimately the person we call God. The truth is as Jesus quite clearly stated to the Samaritan, the non-Jewish woman seeking a miracle that He, Jesus, came only for the lost sheep of Israel. The name Israel in Hebrew literally means: 'arm of God'. So Jesus came exclusively only for these people? It seems to me another dilemma exists or does it? We would clearly have to call Jesus or the authors of the New Testament, liars. Another Samaritan woman seeking a miracle likened herself to that of 'dogs licking the crumbs that fall from the masters table' (Matt.15:27). Jesus was clearly moved by her faith and afforded his healing power to her sick child, a power, which was originally given only to the lost sheep of Israel.

Looking at the other Samaritan woman, at 'Jacobs well', he met very early in his ministry here on earth. There is no doubt that Jesus' intention was always to eventually expand his message beyond the confines of the Jewish people. We know this because he stayed two days in the house of this Samaritan which was most certainly a clear deviation from traditional Jewish faith. Yet Jesus proclaimed quite clearly even to this woman, up-front, that 'Salvation is of the Jews'.

Paul formally Saul spoken to and appointed by Jesus along the road to Damascus, was commanded to preach the message of the risen Jesus to the Gentiles. Well it could be easily argued that Paul was the thirteenth apostle, the one to replace Judas, and not Matthias chosen by the remaining eleven by the casting of lots. The reason why I say this is because one thing all Apostles have in common is that they are personally chosen by Jesus himself. This same Jesus also personally supports his chosen with oracles of the word and real miraculous powers from above.

Again here we see a clear and direct intention to preach and reach out to the Gentiles. This is true but I don't think it was ever Jesus' intention for the Jewish texts to be bastardised and used to manipulate people and the nations. The message for the Gentile has always been a very simple one as spoken by Jesus himself to the Samaritan woman 'salvation is of the Jews'. Does this same Jesus the Jew and proud of his Jewish ancestry somehow and amazingly change into this neon illuminated superstar of the Gentiles allowing his own words to be spread around like a common dip. I don't think so. To my understanding this same Jesus was angry when his father's house was being defiled by money changers, made a corded whip and chased them from the temple court yard awhile angrily overturning tables.

I have deliberately used the word angry because while it is well known that Jesus was gentle and a person who possessed an array of idealistic human and Godlike qualities, righteous anger was of them. It is well known that God is a God 'slow to anger'

(Ps.103:8); yet can be very angry indeed as shown with the flood and the devastation of Sodom and Gomorra by fire and brimstone. It is also written in about whom the rejected keystone falls upon will 'grind him to powder' (Matt. 21:44; Luke 20:18).

Paul is the most important person besides Jesus himself to the Gentile non-Jewish world. To us few human beings who are desperately licking the crumbs which fall from the masters table, Paul's words as spoken by a true apostle and warrior of truth, reveal to us such wonderful promises; a clear invitation from a loving God who is truly seeking communion and fellowship with his most beloved creations.

Before we can even begin to even walk with God one must realise from where one has come. While most people wouldn't even allow themselves to think in such a lowly state; the truth is no one on this earth will enter through the gates of heaven unless they come to terms with where they really stand in front of God as a Gentile or if applicable, as a Jew.

For the Jew it is simple, to accept the Messiah as coming to his chosen people as foretold and proclaimed by the Jewish apostles, such as Peter, John and including Paul who was both Roman citizen and Jew. For the Gentile it is also simple to listen and humbly consider the invitation and message of salvation as proclaimed by the Jewish sect leaders.

I am not sure if the people of this earth really understand the true depths of love that God has for the Jewish people. It can be a very difficult concept to fathom; but if you take the time to contemplate and consider a few facts it is possible to maybe touch on the true extent of this amazing love.

To begin we must consider God's original plan which again is difficult to comprehend as we only have inspired texts and our own physical world around us as a reference. It seems to me that the plan was very wonderful for creation and we sadly are only witnessing a remnant of what could have been.

After 'the fall' I wonder will the world ever know the true sadness and grief that the Creator would have felt having made such a beautiful plan for creation never did he ever imagine that rottenness would be found within. If he knew that his most prized angel adorned with so many beautiful gifts would betray him he would not have allowed him to walk among the fiery stones, a most sacred place with God, as described in chapter 28 of the book of Ezekiel. Lucifer was also described as the cherub that covered the altar of God which was a very privileged position indeed.

It is clear beyond measure that in God there is no such thing as evil or impurity as the creator alone was able to possess and comprehend the knowledge of good and evil. For God the Creator it was not a problem to possess this knowledge; but in His immense goodness and wisdom He was able to know its potential problem for us; the created. It seems to me that God originally created human beings as Gods themselves each with their own freedoms and powers and special colours. Jesus is quoted as supporting the scripture which says 'you are Gods' (John 10:34); implying that we are all gods, as such, with predesigned abilities to voice and act. So we can only imagine what fantastic powers and wonders were made at our disposal in our original design to be regarded as Gods ourselves?

I am sure that within ourselves we somehow sense the shadow of these things as true; well at least I am sure the ancient Greeks did, with their belief in many Gods commanding different realms of the world and underworld.

So here we have God's wonderful plan of creation and then 'the Fall'. It is written that one third of heaven was cast out of Gods presence to their new abode; our earth. No-one really knows the actually time or even the number maybe it is hidden within the sacred texts. It seems to me that judgement of heaven and earth happened at around the same time when the earth was chosen as the place to jail and now holds the condemned spirits of the universe, including us. What was the actual number that fell? Well who really knows what one third of heaven would be but I have a feeling it is a very large number indeed.

Strange how we live in a world which we share with Lucifer, all fallen heavenly beings and all of the human races of the earth rejected from God, cast out, for all intensive purposes, rejected.

Can we believe the parable that Jesus taught when he spoke about the good and bad trees being cut down. Or John 'the Baptist' who stated openly that there is an axe laid at the foot of every tree. To me again this says quite clearly that we human beings are currently in a process of being cut down. This process which involves removing our eternal status from heaven and earth which of course is all owned and controlled by God.

I have within myself a heart, emotions and feelings. I can assume that the Creator also possesses these things of course at a much more 'higher' and sophisticated level; nevertheless he possesses feelings, for this I am sure. It would be impossible to comfort the anguish and pain that our Creator the 'Father who art in heaven' must feel and still feels at the loss of such a magnificent plan and abandoned creation.

As Jesus sat with his disciples on the Mount of Olives projecting his thoughts into the future he shared with them a time coming upon the earth so evil and filled with terror that God will have to intervene to shorten the days that only a remnant can be saved. When we ourselves look back into history we also see great horrors, brutalities and injustices. The question to really ask here is: who in the end carries all the pain of all this? Is it us? Is it nobody? The answer must be God the creator and father of all creation must alone taste and feel it.

All I know is this: God our 'Father who art in heaven', must possess such a sadness, disappointment with a multitude of pains and broken feelings unsurpassed by anything ever created or hoped to be created on the face of this planet. We in our humble little lives experience so many losses such as belongings, houses, lands, nations, marriages, children and jobs;

but nothing could ever compare to the loss or feelings of loss tasted in all its entirety by our heavenly father. To overcome this extreme mountain of evil, suffering and disappointment and then continue to give must come from the greatest heart of love imaginable.

Just because God appears to be distant and far away from this world people forget that He who made the heart to experience feelings of love and joy has the biggest and greatest ability to feel of all. Not to ignoring special people of the earth such as Enoch, Elijah and Moses. What I read in the scriptures is that at least one human being was able to please God completely without exception or concession and now comforts the Father in the depths of his unknown anguish; that is of course Jesus.

Jesus is described as 'a man of sorrows, and acquainted with grief' (Isa. 53:3). Great knowledge of something can be a wonderful thing to possess but it also carries with it a heavy price:

> For in much wisdom is much grief, and he who increases knowledge increases sorrow. (Eccl.1:18)

Those of us here on the earth who are burdened with this most treasured gift enjoy the channels of its dimensions but the price can also be very high indeed. The happiest people on this planet are the people who live a simple life and take each day 'as it comes' living it simply and fully as possible. Not considering the past or tomorrow as Jesus also advised, '…for tomorrow will worry about its own things' (Mat 7:2). I am sure He [Jesus] was well aware of this and made it clear that He Himself was to be burdened while leaving the rest of us to live under the umbrella of this great sacrifice to become as 'little children' innocent in the knowledge of evil but well acquainted with what is good.

The Jewish people were always a special love to God and it can never be assumed that we Gentiles understand or comprehend the minutiae of this great love. What we know from the readings of the Bible is that God didn't choose them for any particular reason, he just chose them. Today as one looks upon a couple of blind lovers, it can appear to be silly or even stupid. Love is like that, it has its own form of stupidity or rather childlikeness which is one of its encompassing attributes which bears little value in today's materialistic world.

Just as David wouldn't kill King Saul an 'anointed' of the Lord, even though he was his arch enemy throwing spears at his head and plotting his murder. He rather and correctly showed reverence, respect and honour to the first love and 'anointed' of the Lord. I mention David as it is written that he was a man after God's own heart and it is for sure that this attribute was one which reflected God's own.

Despite the recorded failings towards God by David and the Jewish people, never underestimate the secret love and passion God has for his beloved people. Who have strived and wrestled with him day after day, night after night and into the early hours of the morning from the very beginning and even to this day.

At what I call, the 'meeting at the well' early in Jesus' ministry, He met a Samaritan woman. God's intention was always to extend beyond the boundaries of the Jewish race as he stayed two days in the house of this woman which was a deliberate and obvious deviation from Jewish practice at the time. While physically siding with this Samaritan he still plainly and openly declared that 'salvation is of the Jews'. Hidden within Gods plan through the revealing of his word was a desire to reconcile with all of humanity, starting with and ultimately to end with the Jewish people.

God chose to become as a Jew and to align himself intimately with the Jewish race. This must never be forgotten or ever ignored as nothing. Salvation is a very delicate and sensitive thing. If one thing is not right one blemish is out of place it is unacceptable. When God gave any instructions either by his own voice or the voice of angels they were always very detailed and precise.

Because of the slackness and weakness of human flesh we just cannot fulfil all the specific requirements as demanded from God and actually because of this we are in a bit of trouble. Yes Jesus comes into play here but the problem is: it isn't just good enough to say the name of Jesus and sit back and enjoy a type of joy ride. The first protocol has to be to seek out the Father.

A path does exist which involves another person carrying the burden of all the laziness, sins and ignorance of the flesh but it is negotiated directly with the Father in union with the Holy Spirit. In all this Jesus the Son of God is the key.

First he lowered himself to the fragility of human flesh into a nation already oppressed by the might of Rome and furthermore into a poor underprivileged family with limited resources and with no land of their own. The family was forced to work a craft of wood which was by no means easy or a lucrative profession. He was also burdened with the heavy rituals of Judaism with all its man made oddities and religiosity.

The journey of Jesus was always the most difficult of any that could ever be undertaken and the cup that he prayed the Father, if it were possible for him not to drink, was a lot more bitterer than the vinegar that he was forced to drink at his crucifixion. The main reason being, there was both a physical component and most difficult of all, the spiritual. I am not saying that being tortured or weakened from hunger or mockery would be easy; but compared to the spiritual bombardment by Satanic forces and in the end, rejection from God himself, to be lowered into Hell, raised and then to continue on with his work even to this very day cannot be easy at all.

As described in detail, by angels [implied] in the epistle to the Hebrews, Jesus is now atoning for sins sprinkling his own blood at heavenly times and seasons within a heavenly temple, performing special rituals of atonement as the priests of the earth even today mimic. The biggest work that Jesus is doing is really to plead day and night to the father for those privileged few who have been given to him who are being transformed and prepared for eternal life. God is aimed and ready to strike the earth with a curse because of deteriorating father and son relationships on the earth as is written in the last words of the Old Testament (Malachi 4:6)). This curse was illuminated in the ministry of John the Baptist extending on to Jesus who is a true personification of a son whose heart was turned to his father. Who was in turn acknowledged by his father as such at his baptism.

  To expand the thinking of this very important relationship between father and son, there is no doubt, that in the creation of the family that God had a special purpose and plan behind it all. I am not sure what the fullness of this plan was but the connection was always meant to be more than just of the flesh. When a son deceives his father to gain advantage it is almost acceptable as in the case of Jacob. If a father was to deceive a son then we would truly live in a most darkened time, there would surely lay a most terrible curse.

3

Kingship

Human beings just love to be kings and to make kings. It is no big revelation for me to discuss a topic which is widely well known in its erroneous ideals already exposed for hundreds, possibly thousands of years. Yet it is covered in this book because it is becoming tiresome I am sure, even to the heavenly Father himself, let alone the poor people who continue to suffer under this delusional regime of safety and counterfeit prosperity.

From reading the thirty-nine Old Testament books we readily learn about the futility of kingship with all its bloodthirsty false symbolisms and declarations of power, coupled with 'create as required' legislation and totalitarian governance of the populace.

From the beginning, kings, thrones and such were not something which God himself taught or guided the people of the earth to follow. Kingship and the lineage of David, a clear directive from above, was something which occurred at the end of this age and from its very infancy was plagued with the usual forms deception, trickery and of course bloodshed.

Where did this recipe to declare 'oneself' a king or kingdom actually come from? The earliest writings and instructions provided by God to Moses gave no provision or recipe to appoint a king or Kingdom. All governance and management was done by carefully appointed judges and of course the Prophets. Not to go into the endless pages of requirements and conditions that God demanded to be met let alone the presence of a volatile Creator who was ever ready to punish quickly with plague, fire and the sword. He was also continually in argument and discussion with Moses, obviously very sensitive in opening himself to a people who had little realisation or understanding of why the earth was created and the extent of the human and heavenly fall. They as a people often failed to realise that they were dealing with the creator of the universe with all his glory, magnificence and power.

I in no way want ever to diminish the magnificence and the enduring importance of the chosen people and have no doubt that if I was to be alive at the time of Moses I would have easily found myself under the Red Sea or devoured by the earth in Gods wrath against my own rebellion by the very presence of my ungodly flesh. God had his reasons to choose this people who were never a people who started with Abraham as homeless nomads who eventually settled in the Land of Canaan which he was to share with the Canaanites.

With all the detailed instructions given to Moses in his books there is no mention of appointing a king. From reading the Old Testament writings and history itself, kings and queens seemed to simply appear from thin air. From what I can read peoples or societies seem naturally compelled to appoint one person as a type of personification of themselves and society. By ceremony a person is transformed into a level of power which usually takes the form of an acceptable dictatorship. If this dictatorship is extended in time and purpose history tells us that the individual then moves on to declare one's self as a type of God. Again we can go back to Eden and the serpent promising Eve that she would be like God. This promise was in fact fulfilled but in such a sickly state that compared to true Godliness it is like comparing a wart to an apple.

Well after Moses' death Israel was governed and guided by Judges and the prophets. Samuel was both a Judge and a prophet regarded as one of the most significant as he was very close to God in a personal way. The time of Samuel also marks a kind of transition away from God and a new way of man which continues well into today's world. It was always Gods intention to directly govern and guide his people himself with the aid of his inspired people. When Samuel grew old his household and all Israel together with their behaviour began to deteriorate. They increasingly pleaded with Samuel for a king. A king was what other nations around them all seemed to possess and it appeared to bring these societies wealth and a united purpose.

When Samuel inquired of the Lord, His response was not good. Yes he could go ahead and appoint a king but it would be regarded as turning away to another God; a brazen form of idolatry. Reluctantly Samuel anointed a king who was called Saul, but God already knew what the future would bring and by the very virtue that a king was appointed meant that God was always now second choice to his people.

*Rejoice greatly, O daughter of Zion! Shout, O daughter of
Jerusalem! Behold,*
*Thy King cometh to you; He is just and having salvation,
Lowly and riding on donkey, A colt, the foal of a donkey.*
(Zech. 9:9)

This 'second place' God came and presented himself to the
people and the earth exactly as he was regarded, always as their
last choice, yet nevertheless a choice. I am sure that even in
God's great wisdom and mercy if the people of Israel followed all
they were suppose to do it would have led eventually to Jesus
naturally taking his throne even on earth. Forces of division were
already seen even in king David's reign and no doubt in time
took a perverted path leaving Joseph and his household far
away from ever being in line for any earthly throne.

4

The Place called Hell

Well, I think its time to talk about a most serious and important subject, that is, to talk about salvation from our mortal sinful nature and our own rejection from heaven itself. I have heard it said that Jesus spoke more about a place called hell than heaven; but this is of course not the case as a simple concordance check will reveal. All I know is Jesus spoke about Hell as it is something very serious for us humans to consider and for us to be aware that it is waiting for a very large number of people past, present and of the future. I also know that using the name of Jesus is not a magic 'get out of gaol card' but we all need to take this place very seriously indeed.

Yes I will talk about the plan for our salvation but we are now talking about reality and the bottom line being that of truth. Why is it so important to consider the place called hell? Well Jesus spoke about such things telling us the story of the rich Judge and poor beggar Lazarus but also we have many examples of Jesus rejecting the rich man who was a reverent follower of the Ten Commandments; but was turned away from eternal life. So where did that man end up if he failed to follow Jesus' guiding words. The place is called Hell; I don't read in the scriptures any other place that he could be going after choosing wealth ahead of salvation.

Human beings like to glory in themselves but we are not as high in the spiritual world as we would like to imagine. Where do we as human really stand when even the unclean spirits of the earth readily recognised Jesus declaring him, 'Jesus, Son of the most high God?'(Mark 5:7), and Jesus' own disciples barely recognised him on their own as anything other than a teacher and miracle worker.

When Jesus was crucified (and rejected by his father), he suffered exactly the same fate that most of us human beings suffer, once killed he went to Hell, spending three days ministering to the souls there before Noah's time. So where was this place? It seems to me it was Hell. When Jesus was resurrected he told the first witnesses of his resurrection not to touch him as he was not yet ascended to the Father, His spiritual garments were dirty from being in Hell.

As part of his work He was placed also into the chambers of Hell and was covered with all the filth of that place. To my knowledge and understanding I don't think a person or human soul exists that once condemned to the chambers of Hell can be released from that place. But Jesus was the first. It is easy to talk about these things and say "well He had this power and he was just doing his job" its easy to talk, but to taste I don't think it is at all nice.

Yes people can mock and laugh at the name of Jesus but this man was the only human being to have entered into this place and ascend again. No doubt the souls before Noah's time would have yearned to be free from their hellish prison but there was nobody to come to their aid, not a soul in four-thousand years. Of course since that time over two-thousand years ago now, I am sure human beings associated with Jesus and know him quite intimately may have also made this journey to that place and were able to also descend and ascend out of that horrible filthy place, at least in the spirit.

What comes to mind is Jesus' preaching in the temple explaining how the Jews talk about Elisha and other historical men as if they are their personal hero or connected to them in some special way? Yet during that time there were many people who needed cleansing from leprosy but only two people were actually healed while the vast majority of leprous Jews lived and died without ever being healed.

It is the same with the modern evangelical churches of today. Everybody knows Jesus and is healed day and night to the point that at times it appears that all sickness has been driven from the whole world by the mere mention of his name. The truth and stark reality is a different matter completely. Jesus and his disciples do in fact heal but as in the times of old it is only those approved of the Father that are truly healed and it is only in very exceptional and rare cases indeed.

We learn a lot about this place called Hell of course in the teachings of Jesus and it appears when you read his words that it is a place he really wants people to avoid as it is a place filled with a fire which to some is an eternal torment. Jesus was God and was fully aware of this place as it was a place created for Lucifer and the other 'cast out' heavenly beings to be tortured day and night. No doubt he has great compassion for us human beings who seem to continue life in a type of slumber believing that all is well and that somehow as night follows day all will be fine even when we die.

According to Jesus Hell is a place to be avoided at all costs and he painstakingly tried to explain that there is an eternal wrath of God against all lovers of wealth and richness and to all those who do not convert and change direction towards what is right especially towards the poor and afflicted.

There is a specific warning to the entire world to those who do harm to children and those who are vulnerable and lesser in our society: 'It would be better for him if a millstone were hung around his neck…than that he should offend one of these little ones' (Luke 17:2). It doesn't matter if you are part of a government organisation, corporation harming children or even solo, the result will always be the same; serious eternal consequences where: 'There will be weeping [crying] and gnashing [grinding] of teeth' (Matt 8:12). There are at least seven references to this 'gnashing of teeth' but it is not appropriate for me to enter them all here.

Many people read the Bible and these words everyday but somehow they are glossed over, I have heard people say: "God is love and would never do such things as to torment people in such a horrible way!"

This statement could be true yet somehow it appears that the consequence from being 'cast out' from God, so to speak, is to be in a type of torment. Isn't the curse of daily toil and childbirth a type of torment already? A prisoner who is confined in a cell even if he has food and good conditions is in a form of torture and he cries out day and night to be free.

I think Hell is a type of reality or truth which our slumbering bodies no longer care to acknowledge (all we have is truth and the reality of our eternal existence and distance from God). Maybe our bodies are a type of delaying shield that is postponing to a degree our inevitable destination. Without intervention and clear change this place awaits the majority of mankind: 'wide is the gate that leads to destruction, and there are many who go in by it' (Matt. 7:13).

I don't want to sound like some disparaging evangelical preacher imposing negative and abusive ideals on to you. I only want to talk about the reality of this place and highlight that Jesus was clearly concerned about it and so we should be also. We shouldn't be scared to face up to the reality of it's existence and never underestimate the promises of extreme suffering this place offers all who make no effort at all to 'repent' and lay down a saving path of good works away from this horrible place.

5

A Sickness called Sin

It is very hard for an individual let alone the whole human race to accept that it is plagued with a type of sickness called sin. What also makes this reality difficult to fathom is the fact that the vast majority of people themselves don't realise that they are sick. To those who do eventually come to a realisation of sickness they often feel alone, isolated and abandoned because everybody else around them seems to be on some heavenly boat ride. To further complicate the situation we live in a world that needs to categorise everything. To realise that you are sick is in itself regarded as a form of insanity or mental illness.

When we talk about the earth and our sinful or 'fallen' condition we often ignore the rest of God's wonderful creation. Sadly they are undoubtedly linked to us and are indeed suffering exceedingly at mans cruel hands. Time itself is a wonderful story teller and illustrates a clear deterioration of man and, sadly, animal kind.

Read how a sixteenth century architect, Andrea Palladio writes about designing religious edifices in the preface of his book:

> *If we consider this beautiful machine of the world, with how many wonderful ornaments it is filled, and how the heavens, by their continual revolutions change the seasons according as nature requires, and their motion preserves itself by the sweetest harmony of temperature; we cannot doubt, but that the little temples we make, ought to resemble this very great one, which by his immense goodness was perfectly completed with one word of his.*

(Palladio 16th century)

Man today even at his most inspired moment would struggle to emulate the sound wisdom, purity and poetic beauty of these words written by this man 400 years ago. How has all this deteriorated? Why does the earth now grow old and tired like an old coat? The answer is sin. God stated if you eat the fruit from the tree of Knowledge 'you shall surely die' (Gen. 2:17). At 'the Fall' sin was discovered and the process of death started immediately with Eve soon after enticing Adam. Even though, the earth itself is innocent, dominion was given over it by mankind and the subsequent destruction is occurring under our very eyes at an accelerated pace all for the love of mammon.

Not to enter the realm of government hypocrisy; but it is obvious governance is all to put on a spectacular show of caring for the people and environment; in reality do nothing except to place increased burdens of regulation where possible to oppress the already oppressed.

Sin is a word in the English language which immediately attracts a multitude of associations such as vicious, evil, condemnation, death, wickedness, badness, destruction and of course judgement. In reality sin is a very difficult thing to pin down and as the apostle Paul stated in his writings about food that what is sin for one person is not necessarily sin for another. When reading the Old Testament books it seems there are just too many sins. The first associated with 'the Fall'; but what followed was an orgy of sin.

The reality or truth about sin is it is something which directly hurts God in ways that we do not fully understand. The heavenly beings thrust to the earth many thousands of years ago brought with them fantastic knowledge. This knowledge of course guided man in building and other enterprises but sadly provided understanding and more intimate knowledge of ways to hurt God. As these beings were once in heaven they were aware of, 'the other world', so to speak.

At the time of Noah, sin was rampant, even the sons of heaven took earthy women as their wives and offspring were also produced. Because of this specific sin the human age was reduced from just fewer than one thousand to a meagre hundred-twenty. It was more the type of sins that humans were doing that forced the Godhead to take the drastic measure as it did and to then go on to flood the whole earth with water.

With a remnant saved and man's age reduced humans continued to slip back into habitual sin. First the tower of Babel came then the demise of Sodom and Gomorra. While God was destroying these evil cities he was also teaching Abram to have faith, to learn how to wait and also trust in a 'living God'. Not turning to idols and instant pleasures of sin but taking that extra 'step of faith' required to form a living and active relationship with God.

Later with the help of Moses God took a closer step towards the ignorant people of the earth and tried to educate humans exactly how he wanted us to live on the earth. Page after page of intricate detail of what is sin and what should follow every trespass. It also instructs on the appointment of priests and Judges to act on behalf of God judging and guiding his people. It was not an easy time for both God and of course the Hebrew people.

One interesting story exists with God present on a mountain. It was commanded that a fence be built around the bottom and whoever passes or even touches the fence 'shall be put to death' (Exod. 19:12). This was a very serious time for the earth as God himself was very close to his creation maybe more closely than anytime since the Garden of Eden. The five books of Moses describe so many deaths and transgressors of the new laws and new way. The time was in fact very brutal and in some ways barbaric. Refinement is a long process and there was no doubt, as it proved that God had a very long and messy job ahead.

When you actually take the time to read carefully the Old Testament books you really could feel sorry for God as you discover just how much effort he puts into trying to educate and refine his chosen people. Then after the rejection salvation is extended to us gentiles and the refinement continues.

Sin must be one of the most difficult and misunderstood words of all time. What makes this word so hard is how can the human race in its blindness and our fallen condition accurately comprehend or understand the entirety of sin to the point that we all can be sinning by just being born into this current world?

The truth is we have no hope really of understanding the entirety of what sin is and actually when you think about things a little better to possess the actual knowledge of sin could be regarded as also a sin in itself. Instructed by the apostle Paul the new Church in Rome was 'to be wise in what is good and simple [innocent] concerning evil' (Rom.16:19). This is a clear progression from earlier humans plunging head first into the knowledge of sin and suffering the consequences. Jesus' emphasis on becoming as little children to enter the kingdom of God, whom I am sure when they are born have little or no knowledge at all of evil or the practice of sin.

It is written that God cannot commit sin. In heaven is no sin. What was once unclean was very quickly removed. Jesus was also very firm about sin. After his healing of the lame man he told him to 'sin no more' (John 5:14). It's interesting that he would command such a thing but he did and was very firm about it. He also spoke that 'if your right eye causes you to sin, pluck it out' (Matt. 5:29). These are very strong words much stronger than any earthy law, prison or even the death penalty.

Jesus spoke that it is from within our own hearts all kinds of evil proceeded. It is easy at this point to think to yourself, how can a simple human being pass through all this? In Moses' time it was ritual sacrifice which atoned for sins even unknown transgressions. For Abraham it was his faith in God which accounted for his sins. In reality it is Jesus who is given by God for the atonement of Sins. The actual mechanics of this is a real mystery even for those who are receiving the atoning.

John provided us with three ingredients to sin, which are; Lust of the Eyes; Lust of the Flesh and Pride of Life. These directly align with the Garden of Eden with Eve firstly, desiring the forbidden fruit with her eyes [Lust of the Eyes], then in taste [Lust of the flesh] and finally, once eaten, to make herself like God [Pride of Life] the most extreme form of pride and of course sin.

What is clear from the scriptures is that God from his secret hiding place broods upon the earth looking deeply into the hearts and actions of his creation. He searches earnestly for those who struggle against sin. He watches as certain people resist and fight to do what they do not want to do. Somehow the decision is made in heaven to help this person in their struggle and they are literally given Jesus. His blood begins to flow through your veins and special holy sinless flesh becomes your flesh, and his bones become your bones. This very moment or second this process starts is what is referred to as being 'born again'. Man in his usual fleshly sickness tries to induce and imitate this sacred and private moment in ritual but the reality how and when someone is born again nobody knows or the exact moment it happens.

Getting back to this 'blood flowing and flesh forming' reference it may be worth noting here that there is a pinnacle moment in Johns [Apostle] account where Jesus clearly and decisively teaches about this even in the synagogue at Capernaum: 'Truly, truly, I say to you, Except you eat the flesh of the Son of man, and drink his blood, you have no life in you.' (John 6:53)

It was after this specific teaching about himself [read slowly from John 6: 26 to 71] that it is written: 'many of his disciples went back and walked no more with him' (John 6:66). It seems to also imply that only the twelve disciples actually remained. This was a very radical teaching and cost literally the loss of the entire mass following at that time; not an insignificant event at all.

It is worth expanding on this very sacred process because many people are really lost here and a great lie continues misguiding thousands and even millions. Standing in an evangelical line or saying some church bred prayer rarely has anything to do with the decision in heaven to make a person born again. All we know is what follows is a final ability to resist the power of sin.

For those who are born again they very quickly learn that things in their lives change drastically. Those sinful cycles finally are broken and two feet are now on the ground again free to walk a path that is seen as right before God. Again the born-again process is only the beginning of a narrow and windy road to eternal life.

Windy because the freed person, although free to walk on a path away from sin, because of the unrenewed mind and flesh often drifts towards its old friend of unrighteousness. The desire is now to do what is right and to regularly seek earnestly to realign oneself on the right path again and again. Past and present sins are forgiven and the consequences of sin and death are taken away. The process of becoming righteous and worthy to enter heaven must now materialise. This final process is '... godliness; and to godliness brotherly kindness; and to brotherly kindness love'(2Peter1:6).

Jesus himself provided direct insights into this process declaring that when the Holy Spirit comes [now present] to the earth:

> *He will convict the world of Sin, and of Righteousness and of Judgement: Of sin, because they do not believe in me; of righteousness, because I go to my father and you see me no more; of judgement, because the ruler of this world is judged.*(John 16:8-11)

It is clear that before this 'born again' condition that the entire world in fact is being convicted or prodded as sinners. For those freed from this burden of sin the process of learning how to be righteous begins, with the sin-cycle broken; righteousness is then a reality. Both the sin and righteousness period occur under the deadly umbrella of Judgement, where Lucifer sits as an ongoing example of having absolutely no hope of redemption ever.

It is total stupidity and in fact a fallacy to suggest that if a person is 'born again' that they are somehow now exempt from judgment. There are many serious warnings to the Gentiles that it would be easy for God to remove the grafted vine and allow the original Jewish root stock to grow freely again (Rom.11:24).

With every mistake the sanctified person in Christ must repent and continue on the journey to become faultless and in fact worthy of this great cleansing process. Jesus is our high priest and is in the heavenly temple at this very day performing the necessary rituals that God requires with his own blood for cleansing and offering himself as the atoning sacrifice.

Holiness or Godliness is a process which must take place which is like a type of sealing of one's body and soul as each perceived unrighteous area is overcome and conquered, figuratively speaking. Righteousness, to a degree, is in our hands but holiness is something which is given as a type of end and rest to our struggle. Sadly, due to our deep rooted sin-sickness, this will be a process which will never totally be over until the very end of our human lives here on earth.

6

Divination and Homosexuality

'Wages of sin is death' (Rom. 6:23), and this death takes so many different forms, all kinds of diseases, sicknesses and afflictions. There is no doubt that our physical form resembles the state of our soul. With a person who departs from evil: 'health to the flesh, and strength to your bones' (Prov. 3:8).

Sin is something which is mainly physically committed yet is also spiritual. There are many types of sin. The most serious according to the scriptures are idolatry, divination and homosexuality. The latter draws the fullness of God's wrath with devastating fire and brimstone. The same punishment appears to be afforded to the ancient Roman city of Pompeii with the petrified remains a continued reminder of Gods anger against excessive ungodliness.

Idolatry is not a topic I will cover in this book but it is worthy of significant discussion and explanation which will be pursued in other writings. We human's literally use idolatry to substitute our personal relationship with a living and unseen God. The greatest Idol of all is our self and the physical objects and circumstances we choose to position between us and our creator.

It is unclear what sins can be forgiven and which is regarded as the 'unforgivable sin' which we are told, in the scriptures, is a sin directed towards the Holy Spirit. Homosexuality may be such a sin as there is no recorded homosexual person in the Bible which was regarded as suitable for conviction or redirection to eternal life. A later section in this book is dedicated to the Holy Spirit and it is shown clearly that her main role is to prepare and 'send forth' Women to be lovers of men. Homosexuality of both men and woman is in direct transgression to this aim and if any person is hovering near this they should be very careful where they are treading.

Sodom and Gomorra where determined to be destroyed when the inhabitants of one of these cities aggressively sought to have sexual relations with visiting angels of God (Genesis 19:5). One of the most dramatic events in the Old Testament is when the twelfth tribe of Israel [Benjamin] was 'cut off' from Israel. A travelling Levite priest was pursued and preyed upon by homosexual men of a town and his concubine [wife] killed (Judges 19:22-27). The whole of Israel were 'as one' nation of God in its decision to 'cut off' one of its own arms as a direct result of the presence of homosexuality in that community.

I want to add what is written here is not a personal opinion. I am only recalling historical facts I feel could bring balance to an on-going debate as our current society desperately uplifts and celebrates what was once accepted as the lowest form of human existence.

Divination could also be 'the unforgivable sin'; but in the book of Acts we read about a sorcerer that was counselled by Peter to walk on the right path but unfortunately to his own demise chose not to heed any guidance. By virtue of Peter's attempt of correction means divination could not be 'the unforgivable sin'.

Sex and immorality is a big issue in this current age and also in Jesus' time. The Samaritan woman at the well was exposed by Jesus to have five husbands and the one she was with was not even her husband. Jesus offered this woman 'living waters' (John 4:10), and with this water she could move on to living a more pure and better life with God and before man. When he forgave the adulteress being stoned it is clear that her sickness may have been much more than the actual act of adultery; but something more deeply rooted. Maybe the adultery was a form of betrayal or rebellion as such against a husband or father who may have forced her to be in a marriage to which she did not want to submit. What ever reason it was, Jesus wanted the woman to have more time to sort out her reasons and live a more honest life in truth and in the light.

Yet to this woman and others he forgave having said: 'go, and sin no more' (John 8:11).The whole purpose of Jesus' coming was to show he carried with him the power to forgive and most importantly to put an end to sin. This was a big claim; but this is what the man Jesus is actually about. Those people that seek to be with him must take this very seriously. It is written clearly and not just once that forgiveness and life with him is an extreme privilege and that every person must examine their own salvation with 'fear and trembling' (Phil. 2:12).

When it comes to divination and homosexuality there is no confusion or 'grey area' to what these sins are about. Society, despite the growing knowledge of the scriptures, seems to be obsessed with touching and even exploring further the endless boundaries of these sinful and dark areas. In the end most people know very well in their own hearts that these areas are wrong but still continue as if on purpose to hurt even more deeply an 'unknown' and 'unseen' God. Consequences are clearly spelled out and the penalty already carved in stone long before the Ten Commandments: the penalty being of course death.

Part Two

7

The Power of Truth

The word truth, the central theme of this book, in itself is truly amazing. For those who understand its power have at their disposal a most wonderful tool indeed. Sadly many people especially unguided religious fundamentalists, most politicians, lawmakers, sales agents, basically any person who wants to manipulate another for personal, social or financial gain will use truth as it can move mountains and even bring down a nation. Lucifer himself also is aware of the power of truth and used it as a weapon at the time of Jesus' temptation, quoting a psalm from the sacred Jewish scripture in an attempt to force him to weaken. The fallen angel was well aware that the songs of David were among his most favourite and treasured words.

It is difficult to draw the line and say that one person has the truth but with the coming of Jesus this all changed. Never before in history has God ever come so close to the world which he had condemned through the ages before. It was indeed a delicate and sensitive time. As since 'the Fall' and abandonment by God of his creation he was still there brooding over the earth but no longer did he walk on it as he did with Adam in cool of the evening in 'the garden'.

From the moment of 'the Fall' the world was set on a dangerous course likened to a ship abandoned and heading towards the rocks. It was not like the story books show a wonderful happy time. Immediately Cain killed his brother in an unprecedented act of violence and hate. This same hatred and violence continues unimpeded rampaging upon the earth as the waves of the sea tear apart the fragile hull of our soul and flesh. The world was on its own course for many thousands of years and during that time God still at times drew close to his creation where he could. Enoch is a living example where he walked with God and as such 'he was not; for God took him' (Gen. 5:24).

I am sure when God created all of mankind, as described in the book of Genesis, his intention was not to create a brutal world filled with hatred, violence and injustice.

The ancient Jewish scriptures really only describe the history of the Jews with a short mention of other peoples and tribes. When Cain was sent from his family with a mark on his head, it is clear that there were other tribes existing. It is unclear how they were positioned in the fall or Gods plan for the world but it seems they were already used to killing and acting in a brutal nature. For this reason God saw the need to place a mark on Cain's head as a sign and a warning to others not to kill him as they would obviously normally do to strangers that wandered from tribe to tribe.

Maybe God had a plan for these many tribes of the earth for them to eventually develop a relationship with God independently, in their own way, unpolluted by the mixing of other tribes. Who knows maybe they all experienced a simultaneous temptation and fall from Grace unrecorded because of ignorance. It seems to me that all peoples of the earth from every tribe of today in some way relate with the story of the temptation and the subsequent fall from Grace. These I am afraid are simply one of the mysteries which we will never know until we enter the next world or an angel of God is given permission to reveal these truths to us.

I often consider the Ancient Greeks how on a small number of tiny Islands true intellectual and analytical thought was developed to such sophisticated levels that is unsurpassed even by our greatest thinkers of today. How did this happen? Where did the ideals and mathematical concepts and theorems come from? As if from thin air so to speak. It is also interesting how it was 'the Greeks' where the Apostle Paul was received most readily on his maiden mission. It could easily be argued that the Roman Empire, having brutally conquered Greece, then went on to make use of its new found treasures of truth, incorporate them into their own barbaric empire.

The tower of Babel is a significant story in the Bible. This was a time just after the great flood where all the people spoke one language. To also build a tower which rose into the clouds and touching heaven itself was indeed an amazing engineering feat even for builders of today. But for these supposed primitive peoples the knowledge to construct such a building must have come from somewhere. It can't come from God directly as why would they have seemed fit to destroy something which was guided by themselves? The tower must have been built under the guidance of another knowledge or source.

Noah and the construction of his ark is well known and documented as being guided by God himself for the purposes of salvation for Noah's family and as many animals as he could save in his boat. This occurred prior to Babel and in fact it was written that all the people of Babel were descendants of Noah.

Throughout this book I speak of 'the Fall'. What is significant about 'the Fall' is one third of Heaven was cast down to the earth. I am sure that the cast out angels and heavenly beings possessed immense knowledge and a multitude of powers. You cannot be part of a world which is beyond comprehension, the altar of the universe, and not possess powers and knowledge of dimensions unknown.

I am of the opinion that many of the wonders of ancient civilizations were constructed under the guidance of these fallen angels and heavenly hosts some of which we now call demons or ghosts which wonder around and co-inhabit our earth today. Just as here on earth we have higher persons who have great responsibilities and the humble that resist the prideful brutalities of the ambitious.

When these beings were cast out they may not have been aware of their fallen state but because of the immensity of their heavenly powers felt they were able to develop and construct edifices which in a way could somehow overcome their fallen position. When God spoke to the serpent, cursing him below the cattle or any created thing declaring that we would crawl on his belly, it is clear to me that this is a reference to a 'once glorious' creature that had free reign of the universe itself and clear access to the throne of God. The Devil now lowered below the lowest created creature, awaiting the consequences of judgement; soon to be thrown into a lake of fire, an ultimate end to his existence (Rev.20:10).

Man's fall was never as heavy as Lucifers never the less we have been caught up with his demise and our own curses [Adam and Eve] which is quite a miserable and hopeless situation to find ourselves in.

It's a sad case for us here on earth especially those small children, born filled with a natural and pure joyful enthusiasm for life. This would be perfect in Gods original design of Eden but in this world is very quickly battered and eventually dwindles to a tearful whimper. Once the ways of Satan are slowly learned such as how to lie and deceive, fuelled with secret thoughts of calculations and dishonest transactions, the consequences for sin slowly begin to takes their toll destroying both body and soul, layer by layer, cell by cell.

Lucifer a once glorious eternal being, with free reign of the universe, now abased and subject to the confines of this world now ruling with impudence, power and ease.

We from the earth are so very blessed to have at the end of this age a visit from God's son Jesus, who even the demons marvelled and paid, to a degree, homage? It was always known that this whole earth was the dominion of Satan, his fallen heavenly beings and the human race with a multitude of tribes and tongues. As much as I would love to tell another story I cannot. Just as I would love all the things I have read and seen with my eyes to be different they cannot be. The truth is the truth and it doesn't matter what we say or do to cover up or hide it. It will always stand on its own like a jewel that cannot be changed even by the hottest fire or flame.

It seems a long way to get around to the main point of this chapter being about truth. Well as already stated there are many forms of truth. But we should never confuse truth with knowledge or knowledge with reality. Reality has a lot more to do with truth than knowledge. It is written that: 'knowledge puffs up' (I Cor. 8:1). Clearly this is linked to the forbidden tree in the garden which was the cause of all this misery and destruction. Reality is most definitely more closely linked with truth as is the tree of life which gives us eternal life. Eternal life is a fruit of life giving water which flows out from the tree of life. The reality is you can feel the power of its benefit as you grow and flourish while others around you grow weak and are dying.

When a tree is cut the top immediately begins to die, the leaves begin to grow brown, moisture begins to be absorbed by the air around drawn by the sun and accelerated by the wind. Death is a cruel reality and a truth which cannot be ignored, similarly life, growth and eternal life.

As already stated God is always watching in the distance and will intervene as often as is deemed necessary to insure human beings receive the consequences for our rebellion and sin. Originally our life span upon the earth was quite long up to almost one thousand years. As a result of sin and unnatural relations with heavenly beings, human life spans were reduced by a sizable percentage to one hundred and twenty years. Oh the earth desperately seeks to find exceptions to this set bench mark but as yet "all the kings' horses and all the king's men" cannot put Humpty together again.

Eternal life has its reality and powers all of its own and is clearly something which we human beings have access to again through the workings of Jesus. But this eternal life does not come from this planet and never can as it is forsaken and lost.

As far as truth is concerned it is obvious that it can never really exist in a pure form [on earth]. This is why the words of Jesus are so crucial to providing light to a dark and lost world. Mankind itself is riddled with untruth and a multitude of lies. One third of heavenly beings were cast down to this earth as profane along with mankind, the whole of Creation itself, was cursed and separated from God with the gates of Eden guarded by angels never to be opened again. So the fact is real truth, if it exists, today can never be known in its purest form on Earth. What we consider to be actually truth may in fact sadly be untruth. How do I know this? Well, because of Jesus' own words on this matter.

How this world toils to clean and brighten things up with all its magnificent buildings, the truth and spiritual reality is not such a pretty sight at all. As Jesus walked He saw people dying with diseases and sickness all around him. It is the same today with, of course, some exceptions which exist under the umbrella of mercy.

When Jesus came he repeatedly stated: 'you [us] are from Beneath; I am from above' (John 8:23). The false religious priests and 'dead', as Jesus called them (Matt. 23:27), often tried to question Jesus with what they felt was truth and at times they held in their hands a type of truth; but because of their inappropriate timing and use it was regarded by Jesus as a form of scheming and in essence an untruth. Nevertheless Jesus on many occasions, most likely more than what is recorded, was forced to come up with some well thought out answers to questions which were clearly laced with belittlement and ridicule of his humble message and teachings.

Just before Jesus' final departure He clearly wanted the world to know that His purpose was to bear witness to the truth. The truth discussion was the last formal dialogue he was to make declaring at the end: 'Everyone that is of truth hears my voice' (John 18:37), before silently submitting to his capture and ultimate fate of ridicule, rejection, torture and crucifixion. Pilate then asked the final question 'What is truth?' (John 18:38). This was an appropriate final question from a man representative of the greatest empire of the earth at that time.

Probably no greater scriptural reference or spoken word exists than Jesus' declaration of: 'I am the way, the truth and the life...' (John 14:6), these powerful few words of Jesus were no doubt heard by John [apostle] in his youth, kept in this heart, eventually grown into the living words of his testament. The word truth like no other word is interwoven heavily into his account and is always the pinnacle or cutting edge of every chapter.

It is in John's account that the Devil [Satan] is branded by Jesus openly and directly as being the father of untruth and lies. It may be hard for us to understand this but in heaven and in God's Kingdom, which Jesus describes as paradise, the word lie does not exist. It doesn't exist because the father of lies and all that followed his lies were thrown out of heaven a long time ago never to return.

Jesus did not lie and cannot as no lie can exist in him because he came from this same heaven which is the same even to this very day, clean and unpolluted. Even the people who plotted his death knew this and they continually tested him with tricky questions in the hope that he would make a mistake so they could pounce and tear him to pieces. But in the end when the wolves surround, build in number and continually attack, it's only a matter of time before they get their meal.

8

Rebellion

Oh, how we human beings love to pollute our world. Everybody knows exactly what they are doing from cutting down trees to throwing a piece of plastic to the ground. We have so many pollutions. Make no mistake about it we just love leaving a mess behind for others to clean. It is silly to talk about this issue as it doesn't matter. What is the discussion and who is to blame? In the end it is the individual who must take account of themself and also justify to self and before God every action that is taken. Again from what I have read in the bible, before 'the fall', Adam representing man had the responsibility of caring for the earth and all the animals.

Who knows maybe after the Fall this responsibility was forfeited along with what I am sure was a myriad of other responsibilities associated with God's original plan. With all the pollutions which exist in the world today there is none greater causing more devastation than all combined and that is idle talk, guided by the almighty tongue. James in his letter to The Twelve Tribes of Israel aptly describes the power of the tongue with its ability to bless and curse others who were made in Gods image (James 3:9).

Every person has a right to this earth and we share together darkness and light, air and water and our right to talk or sing and make a noise or sounds in this world. When a person controls his tongue and lives a life of quiet contemplation, it seems to some that this is an opportunity to fill what they perceive as an empty canvas with words of irrelevance and stupidities.

You can sit at cafes and public squares, market places and all you hear is just idle. With the advent of mobile phones the situation has clearly gone out of control with people, upon receiving a phone call, assume that the rest of society wants to share in their lives and conversations.

This supposed freedom comes to the world through the vehicle of liberty and self-perceived individual rights. All of a sudden we seem to have all these freedoms which apparently include polluting ones right to contemplative silence.

It is written that 'If anyone speaks, let him speak as the oracles of God' (I Pet. 4:11). Paul also in his early letters instructed on the issue of idol chatter. He advised that women were not to teach a man or to be busy bodies but to rather learn in silence accepting only the instruction of her husband.

I am not going to argue this particular issue of Paul's; but all I know is he was the most important person to the Gentile world. While salvation was of 'the Jews' it was through this Jewish man and his special communion with Jesus Christ that salvation was extended to include the Gentiles.

The purpose of my beginning this topic with this issue is not to pass on some personal bad experience I have had with over zealous chatterers, rather to use this as a clear example of a disguised form of rebellion and to highlight our obligation to have consideration for others.

Jesus clearly established a template for us to follow when he told the people: 'whatever you want men to do to you, do also to them' (Matt. 7:12). He deliberately made a way out for all of us to follow, shifting the onus onto the individual person to control one's own behaviour, rather than following the glittering tide of fashion or distorted public ideals of liberty and freedom.

Freedom "Freedom to the people!" the mobs yell in the streets as they burn truck tyres and smash the shop windows of small businesses. But their perceived freedom is all but a disguise for the hunger of their rebellious flesh to cause chaos and harm to their neighbour. Rebellion is but a word yet it contains so much hope of harm and hurt to an unknown God and human beings in unmeasurable quantities.

Why did Jesus preach such a radically and precise message of forgiveness, love and good will towards one another. Why did he purposely go against all man-made traditions and institution? Because he knew that was the only way to escape the stamp of our in-bred rebellion.

Jesus was pure, unpolluted and his message was directly against, in particular, the false religious teachers and traditions of the day. He lasted only three years in public life as the forces against him were, and still are, very powerful.

As Jesus preached against these religious leaders they quickly realised their curtain of illusion was being torn down. They instantly schemed together to discount anything at all that threatened their standing in society. Their secret thoughts were of murder to quickly remove what was seen as the source of the disturbance.

These false religious scribes and Pharisees, as they were called, used questions which demanded answers, desperately seeking for the smallest mistake to justify to the people His removal. These religious leaders I believe were and still are today fleshly manifestations of pure unbridled rebellion.

There is no doubt Jesus has a compassionate heart but he is very annoyed and definitely not happy with religious people extending themselves to the point of wearing actual garments of colour to illuminate their proposed spiritual status in the world and universe. All human beings are responsible for their own actions. Every article of clothing, every hat, and every layer of robe, undergarment, shoe or sandal put on in ignorance or deliberately by hand or command is put on before the creator and to the creator we all must answer.

So where was Lucifer in all this? Was he to blame for the actions of these false religious leaders? The answer is no. Although cast down to this world, Satan is already judged and his path is already set. What false leaders and Lucifer share together is common manifestations of rebellion and will both have to answer before the creator.

Paul speaks at great length in his writings about the warring flesh and the terrible struggle that those who seek liberation in the spirit find themselves in. Rebellion seems to co-exist within all our members and is also part of our human condition.

This world from the beginning was always completely lost and bound in this rebellious spirit. In the gospel of Luke it is written: 'Love your enemies, do good to those who hate you, bless those who curse you, and pray for those who despitefully use you. To him who strikes you on one cheek offer him the other also' (Luke 6:27), and so on it goes. In all reality this is just too much; but Jesus clearly set this as the new bench mark of behaviour for all those in Christ to follow and practice everyday.

When you really sit down and think about the reality of this message it seems a form of madness. Institutions and structures are built upon injustices and lies from the blood and bones of the innocent. We live in a world where boundaries of countries, ancient constitutions are protected as holy oracles, traditions of men twisted upon twisted to fit the current tide of man. Every honest person knows we live in a hostile world surrounded by cruelty and harshness. Any form of weakness is pounced upon by surrounding beasts and eventually scattered and torn into pieces.

Jesus knew very well that his words were totally radical and were in time to start a genuine revolution, to set a fire upon the earth, spreading to greet him upon his return. There is nobody like this Jesus, nobody as he was the first. For those who truly follow after him '…we are killed all day long; we are accounted as sheep for the slaughter' (Ps. 44:22). As he sent them out two by two he stated: 'I send you out as lambs among wolves' (Matt. 10:16; Luke 10:3). People who read this book please don't fool yourselves in thinking all is well that the world is somehow different today. This world is violent and cruel towards the innocent because of sin. The 'wages of sin is death' (Rom. 6:23), declared Paul; with every sin committed there comes the deadly cost of death.

Humankind joined together as one in the rebellious spirit of Lucifer. Those who live a life of rebellion and sin naturally join together with him like putting on a favourite old jacket. Blindness and confusion turns to frustration, frustration turns to anger and then violence. People really do not know what they are doing and where they are going.

'Father, forgive them, for they do not know what they do' (Luke 23:34). Declared Jesus, and again 'unless one be born again, he cannot see the kingdom God' (John 3:3). Both these statements clearly tell us that we are blind. This is a serious problem to live in a world of total darkness. Unless our eyes are opened it is clear we cannot see what is really going on. The eyes are an interesting topic in the bible. So much is written about the eyes and we are in fact told by Jesus: 'The light of the body is the eye' (Matt. 6:22; Luke 11:34), modern interpretation suggests that the eye is in fact the window of the soul. An opening or window to our bodies is an obvious entry point for an enemy to enter and attack, and he does.

In this world of multimedia all our senses are exposed to uncensored stimuli; But none more than that against the eyes. How are we blind? It is clear the little children are not as blind as they readily recognised Jesus in the temple crying out, 'Hosanna to the son of David' (Matt. 21:15). The forces of rebellion within us are strong and from our youth we begin to learn the rebellious way with its secret thoughts and deceptive lies; slowly but surely our beautiful youthful eyes become dimmed and we become blind and lost. Blindness is really no joke as our eyes are probably our most important sense, I am sure not only to provide physical sight but also spiritual.

Samuel the great prophet was very close to God, dedicated to the temple from the age of one year old, stated: 'rebellion is as the sin of witchcraft' (I Sam.15:23). It's again interesting to think about the true seriousness of this form of sin and not simply sweep this under the carpet as something which has been somehow resolved in our modern world.

Rebellion if it is in fact 'as the sin of witchcraft' is a serious problem. Just as our 16th century forefathers also thought so with normal town folk turned 'mob' dragging so called witches into town squares, accusing, condemning and executing them all in one day. The problem or should I say, question is, who is righteous enough to accuse and drag us to a burning stake?

Jesus pointed to the answer decisively with the woman being stoned for adultery, the answer being <u>nobody</u>.

The opposite of rebellion is peace and Jesus in his work calls us to be in peace with one another. Before we can truly become peacemakers and to love one another we must find peace in our own lives and settle our own war and rebellion within our own flesh. There is no power on this earth that can help us. All must come from above through prayer and supplication. It is not easy to overcome these things and the disciples themselves also realised the bench mark set by Jesus was extremely hard to reach. Jesus was well aware of this but still pointed to the only answer when he said: 'The things which are impossible with men are possible with God' (Luke 18:27).

9

Satan, what is he?

Not to further dramatise an already exaggerated misconception, what is this mysterious name Satan? Is it simply a created supernatural being or an entire kingdom or world which encompasses everything which is wrong? Maybe it is best to continue ignoring and pass over it as a bad dream.

Satan or the Devil as he is called was not always called these name as at one time this names can be traced back to a single special angel called the 'anointed cherub', before his fallen state, a most magnificent creation. So magnificent in-fact that he was unique and glorious in his own way to the point that he himself believed himself to be equal with God and to this very day he continues this belief.

At one time approximately ten thousand years ago, in context, not such a long time for an eternal being, Lucifer, as he was then called, was a traveller of the cosmos and dwelt amidst the fiery stones at the very heart of God covering the very altar. You can read all about his gloriousness in the Book of Isaiah (14:12-21) and Ezekiel (28:1-19), if these parts have not already been removed or altered in your version of the bible. It is easy to visualise his form as a serpent or wormlike snake creature clearly befitting one who could travel through the universe through the myriad of holes and dimensions which exist there.

While there is a similarity between a snake and a worm in mobility one big difference is the serpent can actually bite and kill you.

All God's creations are always perfect and magnificent until iniquity or sin is found within and then they are automatically cast out from his presence. His great purge is well documented and known by the earth and unfortunately we poor human beings also once ourselves, a unique and Godlike creation, were also cast out even before we had a chance to realise our own Magnificence, special powers and abilities. When mankind was created it was clearly in its infancy and this Lucifer already referred to as 'the serpent' by Eve, wisely and surely sought immediate destruction of us before we could realise who we really were with such freedoms to eat of every tree in the garden, to share ownership in all God possessed and to be like Gods ourselves but I think for real.

Lucifer and God had a special relationship that is only known between the both of them and so it should be. It seems that this relationship even continues at this very moment where it is written some where that Satan calls out to God night and day. We have the book of Job, some may argue a fictional story, but quiet clearly a realistic contemplation with clear and direct correlation with our own struggles against injustice and our own arguments of innocence.

As mankind was created after Lucifer and obviously Adams relationship was still in early evolution with God making him a companion [Eve] who he [Adam] later blamed for coming between God and himself as time had not yet provided another excuse to be used. Yet Lucifer must have had his own relationship with God and obviously it had deteriorated to a serious degree which would have been a horrible concoction of hatred and jealousies with reasons maybe never to be made known. Lucifer made no attempt to befriend Eve or Adam in the Garden as if he did he would have approached Adam together with his wife as a family.

Rather he crept secretly with a clear and purposeful intention to poison and destroy a very juvenile relationship and creation maybe the greatest ever. It's sad and easy to feel sorry for Adam, once a young friend and companion of God, left scrambling, desperate, lost as he found himself trying to explain his mistake to ultimately receiving his rejection and 'the curse'.

Who really knows how long Lucifer contemplated his plan and the true road or reasoning behind his assault to Gods forbidden fruit. All we can deduce is by the time the serpent approached Eve his plan was already in place. On the surface it appeared that the serpent was offering friendship but it was clearly an enticement for her to do something that even maybe he would not dare do himself. At no time did the deception involve forming an alliance or sharing of consequence, rather I think mankind was seen as a type of threat to the wise old serpent.

Back to our enemy once called Lucifer but now called by Jesus himself, Satan. What about Satan where is he? What is he? Well from his personalised curse in the book of Genesis he is a creature not in humanoid form as he was to be lowered below all cattle and below every beast of the field. All the powers he once possessed were stripped so he can no longer travel around the Cosmos; but rather crawls by the power of his belly on the surface of the earth. We know that God set a war between his seed and Eve's seed implying that Lucifer himself has children of sorts. It could be possibly a formulated genetic mutation— or is it a spiritual offspring of unseen spirits and devils which roam the earth, which has been occurring from the beginning of mans creation on this planet?

In the curse is written: 'He shall bruise your head and you shall bruise your heel' (Gen. 3:15). So we are in a type of violent war even to this very day a war between two seeds which is of all the most dangerous as it can become very difficult to realise who actually is the enemy and who is our ally. In any war it always comes down to either two groups or two individuals; those against them, they against us and in our modern world blue against red.

Jesus really helped in his coming not only to shine a light into a world of dark chaos but to encourage us to continue in our struggle against this seed of Satan which from the beginning pollutes our beautiful world. Getting back to this issue of Satan's seed what kind of seed can this be? We know Eve's seed which is her eggs within her clearly enabling the birth of the Jewish race.

Is it possible that this powerful unique creation can actually create a type of offspring or generation of sorts? It must be all the fallen heavenly beings which were caught up in 'the Fall'.

Jesus called some people especially those pretending to be God's representatives 'broods of vipers!' (Matt.12:34). He directly told the religious 'You are of your father the devil' (John 8:44). He even called his apostle Peter once 'Satan' (Matt.16:23).

No doubt all who are somehow captured or deceived by Lucifer become part of his seed, so to speak. It is obvious that Peter who eventually became a powerful worker of God and a true rock of the church was for a small moment in Satan's kingdom as it appears maybe all of us are or have been at sometime or another. If Jesus yielded to his temptation then [God forbid] Jesus himself would have taken his place as part of the Kingdom of Satan.

Jesus set truth as the measuring stick of determination between Satan and God's people. True justice, if it possibly exists in this world, will always be illuminated by the pure light of truth. Wherever untruth exists there you find Satan and his people gathered together as vultures gather around a dead carcass. Where ever truth and justice exist you will find Gods people congregated and you will see them in all their glory shining on earth and also heaven, the true Kingdom of the living God.

As clear as one plus one equals two, Jesus made it very simple for us to recognise the good from the bad— By their fruits you shall know them' (Matt. 7:16) and later he stated: 'for the tree is known by its fruit' (Matt. 12:33). With his pure words we are given a type of criteria or guide to help us find our way through this identity dilemma. Jesus also stated: '…for they [his sheep] know his voice. Yet they will by no means follow a stranger…'

(John 10:4-5). Later he goes on to openly declare: 'I am the good shepherd' (John 10:11). All the children of God know the voice of the good shepherd but to those who are of Satan they remain and live in lies and themselves are swimming in a sea of delusion, continually fighting against the kingdom of God. knowingly and others unknowingly, lying, cheating, misguiding, trapping, deceiving, stealing, coveting and killing; but more focussed on the harmless lambs of God.

Let us look a bit more closely at Lucifer's transformation from the cherub to Satan. I get the feeling from Jesus' instruction about 'Satan casting out Satan' that actually the word Satan refers to a type of kingdom of evil similar to how we would use the word mankind or really we should more correctly be saying womankind.

We did have the prophets to guide us to help us know who we should fight against but then came the greatest prophet and guide of all; Jesus. He really pin-pointed our enemy making it very clear we the good people of the earth have a serious battle on our hands as Satan is a formidable adversary able to devour men woman and children at will.

There is a reference by Jesus just before he was taken up that the ruler of this world will be cast out and in Luke he was quoted as having said: 'I saw Satan fall like lightning from heaven' (Luke 10:18). Obviously weakened no longer commanding his atmospheric rein; but to once and for all crawl on his belly as was in his original curse at 'the fall'.

No doubt prior to Jesus coming to the earth Satan commanded a much higher and controlled reign where at 'the temptation' was able to comfortably offer the entire world and the glory of it to Jesus. Maybe prior to this time Satan had as yet not been demoted to 'crawling on your belly' status, taking Jesus himself to carry out the final spiritual demotion.

All we know is Satan is now truly cast down to this earth and still continues to wreak havoc upon the earth but because of the enduring work of Christ I feel the human race is becoming wiser to his ways and his presence even in one's own life. Principles of Justice seem to exist in varied forms of democratic rule.

General world health has improved with life expectancy doubling in many countries of the world in fifty years. There has been fantastic advancement in knowledge and technology to help man move away from his brutish existence of times past. Despite all the negative points raised in this book there is no doubt that since Jesus came and ascended into heaven the world has improved in a slow but sure rate.

Sadly the cost of all this advancement has been deterioration to our environment yet still as man discovers his mistakes he begins to find ways to reverse and try and repair the damage he causes in his ignorance. Satan is still with us manipulating and deceiving but I feel at much reduced levels from time past. I am not saying that evil is not rampant on the earth which it is; but that Satan is becoming more and more obvious in his activities even drawing universally secular words such as 'big brother' and 'new world order'. People as a whole are still blinded to the direct workings of Satan but they can sense something evil and not right in the world.

Subjection is still achieved by Satan under the cloak of fear. A fear of losing a job, of getting sick, of being homeless, of dying, and a fear of not finding a partner and so on it goes. There are so many fears that I could make a list bigger than the page of this book and still you would find another fear that our modern world lives under.

To answer the question of who is Satan and what is he is difficult as our relationship with him has never been clearly defined. We have never had an opportunity to know the good part of Satan, so to speak, as God once had known him. The die of our enmity was set well before the human race had a chance to develop into its 'God like' status. For those of us who seek eternal life and redemption we can only take a side line view of Satan and continue hastening to the calling and guiding of the 'the good shepherd' which involves total trust and hope against the intended ravaging of a wolf called Satan.

10

Spiritual Warfare

Surely it's time that the truth about spiritual warfare is known to the world. There is no doubt that a transition of human knowledge of this area has occurred over the centuries and even millennia but not a comprehensive standard set.

The majority of old Testament writings are about man fighting against man, mostly concerned with extending and defending borders. While there are many references about spiritual warfare in the Old Testament it is largely hidden within the texts or at the very least usually detached from man of that time. At the death of Moses it is written [implied] that an angel of the Lord contended with Satan for the body of Moses (Jude 1:9). It was written that King Solomon had power over unclean spirits because of his righteousness.

In the book of Job we learn about our adversary, Satan, being very concerned about our destruction. With most people of the world under his sway he was not satisfied. He also wanted Job, one of the most righteous men upon the face of the earth, under his hand (Job 1:10).

When Moses raised his staff and performed his miracles to free his people from the rod of Egypt, Satan was never mentioned directly only that somehow the power of the black art was in their hands, bringing forth a type of magic to challenge the miracles of

Moses. There is no doubt that there was a dangerous satanic battle occurring in the background as Moses struggled to release his people from the grip of Egypt. While Moses spent forty years in the wilderness after he fled Egypt as a murderer, growing and getting to know an 'unseen God', he still had unrenewed eyes and his hands were not able to record the true knowledge of what happened to him and the life he lived.

Moses was a chosen warrior; a man trained up and sent on a mission at 80 years of age (Exodus 7:7). It's funny to mention this here and also interesting to learn that the Apostle Paul was very similar to Moses in that he was originally complicit in murder [of sorts] and also spent many years alone in the wilderness. Three years in Arabia and fourteen years in Syria and Cilicia, being trained up and then sent forth on a mission to free the Gentiles from the grip of Satan.

I dare to say if the story of Moses was written by Paul or a disciple of Jesus it would have been more about Satan and battling his power rather than the stubborn pharaoh of a dying empire which eventually turned into nothing but sand and crumbling stone.

In the book of Acts it is written that Paul [Saul] and Barnabas went to the Island of Paphos where they found a sorcerer. In contending with him Paul spoke directly to him saying, 'O full of all deceit and all fraud, you son of the Devil, you enemy of all righteousness ...' (Acts 13:10). Paul went on to blind the magician just as angels of God did in the Old Testament blinding homosexuals who lusted after them in the city of Sodom.

Here we have a clear deviation from the Old Testament where man was unequipped to confront these forces directly, unlike the angels of God. With the coming of Jesus a new time emerged as Satan was exposed openly as our enemy and also adversary. Without our renewed nature in Jesus we naturally and very quickly fall under Satan's power and control. When Jesus rebuked Peter, who painted a picture of false hope for Jesus' prediction of pending betrayal and harmful end, He stated: 'Get behind me Satan!' (Matt. 16:23).

From what can be gathered from all the scriptures, especially the teachings of Jesus, there seem to be two types of people that exist in the world. Describe as wheat and alternatively weeds [tares] or either sheep and goats. Basically two groups with one destined for eternal life and the other associated with Satan and destined for destruction.

Spiritual warfare as such can take many forms. It is not an easy area to fathom and can take years or easily a lifetime to understand even the most basic principles associated with this world. In the end it is a war and it is on-going. It has no fairness or niceties, only victims and casualties, with blood spilled becoming younger and younger and more innocent. Hopefully we are closing soon to an end to this most horrible battle.

For those who are of Satan and are weeds or goats, there is no warfare at all only a lustful surge towards pending destruction, blinded by the very smell of their own crafty lies and enduring corruption which they spread among mankind as a deceptive disease.

But to the sheep, whom the Shepherd leads, at times it is not so easy especially as one strays from the set path and is choked by the aggressive weeds. Jesus calls himself: 'the good shepherd' (John 10:11) and declared that: 'For my yoke is easy, and my burden is light' (Matt.11:30). The one closer to Jesus is safest on the path towards eternal life.

As far as direct attacks are concerned it is written in the first epistle of John: 'he who has been born of God keeps himself, and the wicked one does not touch him' (1John 5:18). Which is of course true yet Jesus (in his teachings) doesn't even count being killed for the sake of the kingdom of God as Satan touching us.

An attack from an opposition force usually involves three forms, spiritual, physical and emotional. Spiritual is the presence of an unknown force like a wind or gravity which seems to come against us internally attacking a part of us which we cannot feel in our flesh yet is within us forming part of our entity or soul.

A physical attack is an attack directly against our body or flesh. It can take many forms such as sickness, momentary weakness, physical unprovoked bashings, even accidents which cause enduring pain and suffering.

An emotional attack can be the most devastating of all attacks as our emotions control our actions and most decisions we make as humans, being created in the very image of God. Pavlov's dog experiment proved that we humans are very different from the rest of the animal kingdom where our emotions guiding us like a rudder, unlike our animal friends drooling saliva at the regulatory ring of a bell at dinner time.

There is no creature on this planet which kills itself like human beings, often in circumstances' of prosperity and success. The answer to the question why? I surmise that it is a direct attack to the emotions by a satanic unseen force, further compounded by circumstances which frustrate, allowing room for only one apparent solution, that of physical suicide.

Returning to the world of the physical, we human beings are burdened by many physical needs. The need for food and shelter is probably the greatest of our needs and most other needs are associated with these two. On both accounts Jesus preached against these things indicating that we humans are far too preoccupied with food and decorative edifices and we should be more concerned about the things of God. We need to focus more on Justice, Love and Truth.

The greatest thing we actually possess is our own body which is a type of tent which houses our being and soul. Eastern religion has long recognised and embraced the importance of the human body as being a type of tabernacle being sufficient for all our needs even providing us all the nutrients we need for extended periods of time, months or even years.

Probably the greatest assault to our physical body is to be killed. This is what was chosen against Jesus very early on, even before He was born and of course followed Him most of his earthly life. For those few who are also chosen to be on the front line, so to speak, death and threat of death will always be a factor in their lives.

So how does a spiritual attack really occur? If it does exist when would it be the best time to carry out such an attack? Again using Jesus as our example we can learn a lot about this during the temptation of Christ. The very end purpose of Satan's attack was to make Jesus pay Satan homage, to bow down and worship him. This final request occurred after Jesus was physically weakened by hunger and then emotionally weakened by self-doubt. After these two attacks came the spiritual offer of the entire world, in so doing attempting to bring Jesus under his power and control.

The forces of Satan bombard us day and night trying continually to break us down both physically and emotionally. Making us homeless, hungry even after you have worked so hard all your life, day after day, week after week, year after year. We begin to doubt ourselves and our own beliefs and abilities. We are then broken down and down to the point were we are presented with Satan's world in all its glitter and glamour, up to our final surrender. In the end we are spiritually enveloped and submit to his power and control doing what we do not want to do and what we really deep down hate.

For those who struggle to escape this final attempt of spiritual control there is no end to our struggle against him and his forces. You will always fight day and night, until your very end, as to stop struggling is to fall into the cold hard hand of Satan and his kingdom. Paul himself declared that he wished to be absent from the tent of his body and present with the Lord. He was very much aware of the continuing struggle against Satan and his world into which we are all born. To say that this is not Satan's world is to call Jesus and all his disciples' liars almost all of whom died a wicked and cruel death in their own individual fight and in disobedience to the masters of this world.

Spiritual warfare is exactly as the word implies: it is a spiritually experienced war and can easily be discounted by the majority of the world as nothing but a self-induced psychotic episode. But to those who have taken the step to pull away from the grip of Satan in their lives very quickly one realises there is something more going on behind the scenes.

Fear is a big problem in accepting the reality of spiritual warfare because it's hard to see the road ahead as our path is not only narrow but windy. Just as a soldier would prefer to fight in a battalion we naturally find it easier to fight even a spiritual war together with others in a group. Unfortunately while we are in-fact part of a transversal church of believers we must fight our war alone like Jesus did.

Jesus was the first to strive against all the forces which are against mankind and face the darkness of the unknown and succeed. For us to also have eternal life we must follow after him just as all the apostles and others did ending in their own persecution and death. Yes it is easier as Jesus said he would send us 'a helper' and this helper strengthens us, giving us wings and heavenly powers to overcome the full force of spiritual attacks.

To not be in spiritual warfare is not to be a true follower of Jesus Christ. Just before our Lords escorted departure, Jesus said: 'For if they do these things in the green wood, what will be done in the dry?' (Luke 23:31). A clear warning for the future how it will become harder and harder to preach and proclaim 'the way' and true teachings of Justice, Truth and Love.

You may be carried on the shoulders or in the shielding arms of Christ himself but you will always sense a raging battle around you. It is easy to fool one's self into discounting the war as already won but it is a foolish and misguided belief. Warriors of truth are falling day by day and will continue to fall until the very day the Christ returns with all his angels in the clouds and is seen as lightning strikes across the sky. Until then the battle continues to the very end and with this I also say Amen.

11

The Spirit of the anti-Christ

This subject is of all probably the most relevant to this current world and begins with the birth of Jesus Christ. The Angels who appeared to the Shepherds' declared that day:

Glory to God in the highest, And on earth peace, goodwill towards men! (Luke 2:14)

What a truly wonderful and glorious message for the world and a true beginning and revolutionary change to how we as people view and treat one another on the earth. Prior to this time the ideals of peace and harmony were embedded within religious enclosure and ideology, never expanding past the walls of literacy to the universal masses of the earth. For the very first time peace in all its power of solidarity would be born paving the way for real prosperity and human advancement amidst a savage and hostile world

The birth of Jesus was a significant event on the earth drawing three wise men from the East (Matt. 2:1). Wise because they were soberly aware of the signs and fantastic changes about to happen on the earth. Immediately King Herod was drawn into a murderous rage causing Joseph to flee to the safety of Egypt with Mary and the infant Jesus. It is but a story passed down through the centuries by oral tradition but events powerful enough to send shivers down one's spine to think of the vulnerability of one small infant thrust into a cruel and brutal world.

From the beginning of Jesus' ministry he projected the message of peace. His first miracle at the wedding feast at Cana requested by his mother was to peacefully resolve a potentially volatile situation of wine running out at a wedding. The greatest manifestation of his ministry was seen with his now famous 'sermon on the mount', where he declared 'Blessed are the peacemakers, for they shall be called the sons of God' (Matt. 4:9). At his end he asks the Father to forgive the very people who are killing him on the cross knowing full well the wrath and anger of God against those who hurt the pure and righteous. Finally he offers the entirety of his majesty [himself] to the whole world as a living and eternal sacrifice making the way for a bridge of reconciliation between mankind and an angry God.

The gentle spirit of a little child in a manger was carried through every muscle and pore of Jesus' life. Isaiah prophesied of him: 'A bruised reed He will not break' (Isa. 42:3). He was and still is the complete 'peacemaker' accepting always the lowly position of last. It is also interesting to observe how Jesus even before his own disciples portrayed himself not as a strong king bringing forth fire from heaven like Elijah but rather submitting to his captors 'silent as a lamb that is led to the slaughter' (Isa. 53:7). The disciples of Jesus wanted to command fire down from heaven (Luke 9:54), but he turned and rebuked them explaining they were of a different spirit. This spirit was the unique spirit of Christ, one of peacemaker and of course servant to fellow man.

The animal kingdom readily provides ongoing examples of power and dominance. Two horned male animals puff themselves up displaying the immensity of their power, they eventually clash, warring for hours, until one submits and moves away. Human beings also replicate this behaviour extending first into groups and then to whole armies, parading for the entire world to see, displaying great prowess, colour and force.

There was a time that man and God were two warring forces and in a way one finally yielded, this of course was 'the Christ'. What is interesting about Christ is that he is both man and God, yet it was his role as the 'son of man' that made his mission so successful and ultimately a peacemaker.

The spirit that Jesus came with was and is still a stumbling block and an enigma contrastingly going against the very design of nature itself. In Christ we are called to give to those who are in need, to go an extra mile when asked to travel one, turn the other cheek when struck, and so on it goes, all against our natural instincts and pattern of design.

It would be silly of me to repeat all the unique sayings and acts of Christ here yet it is clear that they all pointed to a man who cared about others and wanted us to also follow his lead even if it meant facing death itself. We are in fact called to become 'Christ-like' and this is by no means an easy task especially in today's world where any form of weakness is immediately pounced upon.

After Jesus' resurrection and ascension, the Holy Spirit descended in the sound of a rushing wind and tongues of fire rested upon those gathered. Men spoke in different tongues unlike the time of Babel and its collapsing tower the spiritual force this time was to help heal the divide of language (Acts 2:2-4).

In the earliest gatherings of believers all things were in common and possessions were sold and distributed equally as anyone had need (Acts 2:44-45). There is not a shadow of doubt that the intention of heaven is for us here to live together on this earth in a communal type system, sharing wealth and resources as each group and individual would have need. Where fundamentalists got the idea that wealth and power is a sign of 'being in Christ' is unknown. Jesus never promoted individual wealth rather freely feeding and healing those around him for no charge or implied donation.

The times then were indeed different and the structures and boundaries which held society together were much different. Yet with the birth and spreading of this Christ spirit came what is termed in the bible an anti-spirit working directly against Christ and strangling his simple message of sharing and ongoing concession one to another.

I am in no way supporting any existing communist system of government past or present as these are clearly anti-Christian, atheist, ideological blankets of control and vice upon its peoples. What I am suggesting is that for any system of government to associate it's self with the embodiment of Christ must have some form of socialistic system of sharing lands and distribution of wealth to the needy and poor. It seems impossible to ever have on earth what the Spirit first guided early believers but it must never be covered over, rather it must become an ideal to be pursued with full fervour.

Probably over the last forty years we have seen a dramatic and decisive rise in the spirit of the 'anti-Christ' as it is termed in the New Testament writings. Jesus didn't speak much about this spirit as he was in the process of establishing his own spirit of truth, peace and justice across all the earth. The term anti-Christ refers to any force or doctrine which directly contradicts or stifles the teachings and/or the spirit of Jesus.

It is written: 'Now the Spirit expressly says that in latter times some will depart from the faith, giving heed to deceiving spirits and doctrines of demons' (I Tim 4:1). I have no doubt that the doctrines of demons and deceiving spirits have been responsible for the development of a myriad of cruel and unjust systems in society under the cover of democracy. Unjust systems such as corporations and banks who openly and exclusively by design of their structure, rip natural resources, and gather wealth for a handful of individuals at the cruel expense of the humble individual and worker. These systems generate a mountain of wealth without environmental obligation or social 'duty of care'.

To promote communal living today, especially in the United States of America is to be immediately branded a 'pinko' or an 'unchristian' communist. But I must argue here that the current alternative of privilege and wealth in the hands of a few cannot have anything to do with Christ or his proclaimed kingdom and never will. 'It is easier for a camel to go through the eye of a needle than for a rich man to enter the kingdom of heaven' (Matt.19:24). No doubt the rich and poor divide was just as present in Jesus' time but nevertheless his words still stand and will forever.

A 'real' follower of Jesus can never follow or be a party to the unjust systems of wealth created by banks or corporations and most definitely if he doesn't share as Jesus himself gave example.

I can imagine the excitement of those few individuals in the early days, with unjust systems in place, and the flood of money just pouring in like a river flow. But they were not to know their own souls were being destroyed and their temporary joy will one day be as bitter as gall from the stomach of the humble worker who carried the full weight of payment upon his back with the grinding down of his joints and bones.

It seems clear that as Christ first spread his simple yet powerful message that Satan very quickly moved to start his own fire, so to speak. At every station I am sure once a light of truth begins to shine there was Satan ready to put it out. It has always been this way and will be like this at the very end until Jesus puts a final end to all things.

About Satan it is written: 'Behold, you are wiser than Daniel! There is no secret that can be hidden from you!' (Ezek. 28:3). It is clear that he was wise enough to force Joseph and his family to flee for their lives and raise up Herod to kill all the male children under two years and under in a direct attempt to get rid of just one little child of promise. The spirit of the anti-Christ is as powerful as it was even at the beginning and even smarter and cleverer, driving out and stifling even the smallest movements of 'Christ-like' living.

Even in the wilderness Jesus was held in bondage by Jewish law which forbad him to teach until he reached the age of thirty. Only the family of Jesus knows what other attacks came upon the humble family of Joseph and how often Jesus was saved from the threat of death. There remains a mystery of what happened to Joseph but folk law suggests he died a type of natural death maybe of sickness or old age. I suggest he was attacked by satanic forces both physically and spiritually to the point where he was not around to assist Jesus in his work. The role of Mary his mother also seems clouded and minimalistic she seemed rather preoccupied more with other family members than with the direct mission and work of her son Jesus.

The true spirit of Christ is a brotherhood of men and women working and sharing together giving concession and help one to another. Of course there can never be a heaven on earth but eternal life is the reward which awaits all those who answer the call of Jesus. Compared to all the wealth and richness of this world to live forever and to have an opportunity to continue your being into another world is a most valuable precious thing to all those who realise the call and the promise. There are many forces at work to discount the value of this promise and sadly many people forfeit their opportunity to inherit not realising the true value of the invitation.

12

Man-made Systems and Injustice

Who gives us the right? To use words and images of inspired texts which largely belong to the Jewish people? Who gives us the right to call someone or a group of people, heathen, without a God. Who gives us the right to destroy nations, killing young men, taking their possessions and even their wives? Who gives us the right to take land which was occupied and owned through ancient birthright, enjoyed for thousands of years? The answer to question which asks: 'Who gives us the right?' is <u>nobody</u>.

Democratic government and the process of Government have its roots embedded in Ancient Greek culture and tradition. The barbaric Roman empire very quickly found itself naked and without justification for its brutality and quickly sort refuge within the inspired ancient Greek tradition.

The Romans immediately absorbed the ideologies and images of grandness from the Greeks. While distorting the pure essence of the Greek ideals they tried desperately to align themselves with the honest processes of the democratic voice. The Romans very quickly Inventing tools of exemption such as the Senate, election by committee and the wonderful new exclusive category of citizenship. Where to be non-Roman was deemed to not be part of the modern world, a non-citizen, a simple savage not entitled to the same rights as the rest of the Roman Empire. Notice the similarity to the justification of European empires of conquest?

It is funny how this game of citizenship still continues today, with everybody fighting for the same illusion of freedom, and the simple right just to be. The Apostle Paul himself was very quick to realize the rules and foolishness of this game. He wanted to receive a trial as a Roman, a citizen, rather than a commoner who apparently in that world had different rights of eminent persons associated with the empire of the day. He played the game to effect a more glorious departure from this world and took opportunity to spread the message of the Gospel to the very heart of humanity and the centre of the modern world at that time.

When a person is born into this world he is automatically a citizen of the planet but this form of citizenship is not accepted it is deemed illegal unless one is registered. I have touched on the stupidity and hypocrisy of Government but what to say about the hypocritical stupidity of religion and the religious?

If God in heaven has anything to do with the madness of government and religion that exists in this world today then who would want anything to do with a God like that anyway? But the refreshing truth and reality is that God has nothing to do with the madness and confusion that is apparent all around us today. Actually we can attribute this to Lucifer the fallen being who once occupied the highest post and now the least. It is written that

'Satan stood up against Israel, and provoked David [King] to number Israel' (1Chr. 21:1). The severe punishment by God for this act of 'numbering' by David recorded in 2 Samuel 24:13.

What is really sad and an integral part of our fallen human condition is we all seek for an easy way out of the mess we have found ourselves born into. Man again with his clever devise and fellowship with Satan always seeks to find and invent an easier way to do things. In one of Bob Dylan's [eminent folk singer] songs he says: 'it costs more to store the food than it does to give it'. Over and over man tries to re-design and fix things that don't even need fixing but lacks the faith and true wisdom to know when to leave something alone and just 'let it be' (Beatles).

When considering the temptation of Eve, people forget that Adam was also cursed by God and thrown out of the garden. Since then man has quietly struggled against his curse to toil a cursed land which will bare thorns and thistles all the days of his life (Gen. 3:17-19). A profound quote exists spoken by a former Australian prime minister were he states 'life was not meant to be easy' (Malcolm Fraser). Again the imagery and words lifted from sacred text were used in a clever way to silence 'the critics'.

Another favourite saying often used in man-made courts of law is the classic 'Let him who is without sin cast the first stone' (John 8:7). Courts of Law, administrative bodies, committees, a multitude of peoples just love quoting these holy words and many other inspired words and phrases thinking that some how they are a type of 'get out of gaol free card'. The true essence of these sayings and contexts is against injustice, corruption and dishonest gain.

Injustice is a very valid word and one which God vigorously aligns himself with. In the end the chosen people of God rejected the invitation to the wedding feast. The invitation went out to the entire world. In Matthew's account it is documented in one of Jesus' parables. But while the invitation appears to be an open invitation it is not without its conditions. When the master of the house being God himself attends to meet his guests he finds a man not wearing the appropriate dinner garment and is quickly removed from the table bound and thrown into hell. It is written here that 'many are called but few are chosen' (Matt. 22:14).

It's funny in the Christian world of today that there seems to be a type of misconception that the Jews failed to receive the invitation of eternal life and a wonderful life with God and heaven. This is very false indeed and a serious delusion.

The religious being intimately aware of this requirement of a special garment needed to be at the special feast, very quickly have made their own with such wonderful array of colour and designs. But alas none of these most precious garments woven by the greatest the world can provide will be the right thread to weave the garment of the righteous who will sit at that wonderful table.

A little hint right now if you are one of these people wearing in anyway a cloak, vest or costume that resembles a holy garment that proposes to mimic even in the smallest way a form of holiness of priestly clothing. I can assure you that no place in eternal life exists for you let alone taking part in Gods wedding feast.

The only garments I would suspect could possible exist would be King David and possibly the robes of the high priests before and after who wore their robes honestly and according to all that was written and required by Mosaic law around that time.

I am really sorry to tell you that the Jesus party is over. The time has come for the ignorance and all stupidities to cease. For the elect the only garment that can exist at that special table is the one provided by Jesus Christ himself. Jesus spoke so plainly about his importance and the importance of how only 'He' alone is 'the way, the truth, and the life' (John 14:6). Jesus is the only way into reaching the chambers of heaven, not me or the most prominent apostles or Holy men, but Jesus alone, Him.

To make things even more difficult, Jesus and his apostles had the power to give and also take away eternal life. Ultimately it was the Father from heaven who drew people to his son Jesus and ultimately gives them eternal life. Election is most certainly by grace but let's be honest about this. Salvation is not made until we are actually 'saved' and sitting comfortable at the table of God. It is also written in the letters that we are in the process of being 'saved' (Rom.8:24).

There is no doubt that those whom God has chosen feel the loving and guiding hand of God's spirit but we are not there yet. As I stated earlier Jesus in his short time here on earth once freed from the bondage of the Rabbinical age restriction of thirty was quick to start his fight against injustice. One of his first miracles was to heal the old man waiting near the healing waters and so on. To be associated with Jesus is to fight against the injustices of this world. To be a true brother and friend of Jesus and gain the special dinner garment that is a clear requirement of all invited guests, one must be aligned intimately against injustice.

It's stupid to talk about injustice three thousand years ago in King David and his world. We have to be realistic and realise that we are here in the Twenty-First century and injustice is more rampant than ever before in the history of the world.

Most indigenous persons on the earth have been conquered, their natural resources exploited and then they in humiliation, forced to assimilate, learning the conquerors language and live under the tyranny of rule with a system and way of life imposed brutally and often in the name of God and Jesus himself. It doesn't matter how many times one looks back into history it's always the same old story. Ravage with a gun or sword in one hand and then justify with the Bible or Koran in the other.

When a warrior of truth stands up against the systems and injustices of the day it always ends the same way in a brutal and cruel death. It doesn't matter how history tries to beautify the ugliness of their killing, ether by hanging or a simple bullet. Murder always will leave blood and a permanent stain upon the earth and on the hands of those who are a party to this act. Often I think of how hard it would have been for the apostle Paul, who would have truly lived a tortured life, having once been a condoning killer of Christians then through Christ went on to become one of the greatest Apostles and a true warrior of injustice, especially within the church of God itself.

Make no mistake about it Jesus the man always arrayed himself closely against injustice and any real warrior of truth will always be seen fighting against injustice in the many ugly forms in which it exists, in the past, and predominantly in today's world.

Jesus' main fight for injustice was within the spiritual family or church of God. He wasn't so concerned with the affairs of the Roman world rather he paid respect to the governing empire of the day having said: 'Render to Caesar the things that are Caesar's and to God the things that are God's' (Mark 12:17).

Injustice is an ongoing consequence of narrow-mindedness and a world guided by the blind rather than the Godly and wise. It was unjust that the woman being stoned for adultery was to be killed by secret adulterers and sinners. It was unjust that Jews were not allowed to perform basic tasks on the Sabbath day. It was unjust that the kingdom of God was closed to the unclean non-Jewish people. It was unjust that the poor tax collector was trying to make a living from a protective system he didn't really support in his heart. It was unjust that you had to be authorised by the high priest to exercise spiritual powers and perform miracles of healing to the masses and so on it goes...

Part Three

13

The Messiah, Lawyers and Lawmakers

Its funny but when we think of Jesus and all the writings that we have read about him here even in this book, we fail to forget he was simply a human being just like all of us. He breathed in and breathed out, he had to walk and travel from place to place, climbing up and climbing down, moving forward and coming back, step by step.

It is written that the simplicity of Christ would in itself be a 'stumbling block' in fact to many people in his time, it was. It is well documented that the oppressed peoples in Jesus' time were yearning for a leader, a king, to rise up against the Roman oppressors and rebuild the nation of Israel. For many, Orthodox Jews even of today, reject the creation of Israel declaring that this contravenes the scriptures. It is written in the Old Testament writings that the messiah will come restoring the state of Israel, not man, being in the form of the US and British Governments.

Not to become embroiled in political or philosophical debate, if one truly believes in the scriptures with what was prophesised by the prophets then the messiah has already come. According to the inspired texts the state of Israel already exists in one form or another.

The question to answer here if one wants to be truly honest is how no country of Israel existed for just under three-thousand years (since King David's reign), then, all of a sudden without the showing of a messiah [or Jesus] a country of Israel was created? Well the answer is this and it's the same with most countries of the world they are self-proclaimed and man-made. The boundaries are of mans devising and his hands, not by God.

Don't get me wrong I am not against the country of Israel or any other country for that matter. What I am saying is man has created these countries and the different boundaries. It is truly the highest form of arrogance to suggest that God himself draws lines on a map with his own hand and declares them a country. These have been set by man's hands [lawmakers] for the sole reason of governance with the underlying purpose of domination and control. Oh how man guards these boundaries even giving human life for a few inches of soil!

So if Jesus is in fact the Messiah then Israel of today actually is in existence somewhere and it's not the recent man made country called Israel. If this is the case then where is it? The answer is very simple when you look at the Hebrew meaning of Israel which literally means 'arm of God'. It is a spiritual reference to an exclusive family of God whose boundaries are only known and acknowledged by God himself.

Israel of today is every person Jew and Gentile grafted onto the original nation of people destined for eternal life. It is largely unseen because it is humanly impossible to register such a grouping of people scattered all around the world. Lawmakers have attempted to impose registrations on congregations and religious communities but this is as accurate as registering all people in the world who have a scar on their body. This is impossible, but to God, who has every hair numbered on our heads, not such a difficult task.

Who really is to blame for the design of these strange macro and micro systems of boundaries and controls imposed upon the peoples of this planet? Who is this mysterious group of people interwoven within the fabric of all societies that create all these strange ideas and guidelines? They are the lawmakers.

What is interesting about these mysterious lawmakers is that they are one occupation that Jesus took particular interest in criticising directly. He never condemned the Roman soldiers or tax collectors rather directly aligning this profession with the Pharisees' as types of partners in crime, extensions of corruption manipulating the law to protect those serving them best. Yet not one person, not even in our current world, except solely Jesus himself had the courage to openly and directly attack the very essence of this most evil and devilish profession.

Jesus attributed to the lawyers that they have taken away 'the key of knowledge' and that they have not entered in and hinder those who seek to enter (Luke 11:52), I would like also to add here after the word enter– 'the truth'.

How do I know this is a devilish and evil profession? Jesus declared it so. At the time of his transfiguration a voice came out of the cloud, saying: 'This is my beloved Son, in whom I am well pleased. Hear Him!' (Matt. 17:5). I am sure this means to actually listen intently to his words spoken by this man.

Lawyers and lawmakers of today are no different from that of two-thousand years ago and beyond that. Somehow with the modernising of this world and 'free press' this creepy profession seems to have undergone a miraculous transformation? As far as my historical knowledge goes I know of no such reformation or renewal ever occurring. Rather today lawyers have more power, control and are positioned even more permanently in most houses of parliament and make up a sizable majority of all Governments. Their power base has progressed from being sideline scavengers of the religious, as they were in Jesus' time, to becoming Prime Ministers and now even an elite bread line of Presidents all over the world.

It is truly pleasing that in the short time that Jesus was here, He was able to directly expose and rightly attack the fake religious guides and their companions, the lawmakers.

What is also very interesting is how even the lawyers, when the 'chips are down' and their own resources expired, with the gall of Satan, comfortably quote the pure and powerful words of Jesus who has silenced time after time many a confused court. One of their favourites being 'he who is without sin...' (John 8:7). Well my friends some sins remain and I have no doubt that a lawyer using the very words of a man who himself was vehemently against them is equal to a person cooking a lamb in its own mothers milk.

My answer to examining any law or lawyer is the same measure that Jesus used when he asked them a question. He asked them 'Is it lawful to heal on the Sabbath day?' (Luke 14:3). What I think Jesus is really saying is human beings whom laws are supposed to guide and protect were never meant to cause harm or hardship and most certainly never to hinder or hurt an individual of any society.

I am prepared to concede that there exists a type of lawyer that in fact helps society, but this form is an advocate rather than lawmaker. Advocates become necessary because of the extreme complexity of an unjust system of compounding laws and statutes originally created by the lawmakers. This form of advocacy is also limited usually depending on the availability of large amounts of private money to realise even the smallest form of justice in a sea of injustice.

Oh yes the lawmakers do provide a token form of State or legal aid. But this is operated on a minuscule budget to provide only basic operational service to the court mechanism. This is an illusion of assistance to the people who are forced to carry the heavy burden of ever-increasing laws. These laws are only felt by the very vulnerable of society and usually the most honest of persons.

Lawmakers still remain alive and well today continuing to grow legislating first to maintain their own existence then to leave behind a thorny clouded maze of confusing rules and regulations. These confusing laws are given 'God like' prominence and are guarded as such while human rights, individual enterprise and honourable trading between men diminish day by day.

God please help us from these monsters that prey upon us like vultures who just love eating the flesh of the weak and drinking the blood of the unfortunate.

14

The Day of Your Visitation

Visitation is an interesting word and not one that can easily be ignored. In our modern society unless a letter is registered it can be assumed as having not been sent or received and even then it can be ignored by not being opened. But when someone is visited it is a personal event where in the presence of faithful witnesses no argument could even be held to the contrary.

This word visitation is used quite a lot by Jesus and usually He associates this with a warning signifying a very serious moment or event in a person's life. Important because it is the exact moment when it is decided whether you are suitable for eternal life or eternal separation and condemnation from God and the heavenly family.

It does appear that not all people are included in this category for testing or visitation as some are purely destined for destruction. They are actually referred to as 'sons of perdition'. Again this is really not our concern as all of Creation is in the hands of our creator and it is He who is responsible for his created. We have no right to question or even reason why.

It's actually very simple, if you for a moment are exposed to a holy and heavenly event, how you respond at that moment even if it is for a second or a minute, how you react or respond is how you would react and respond even if it was one-thousand years later. Time isn't what is important with salvation rather it is the moment.

Life is a wonderful and amazing thing but Jesus may only pass by us once in our lifetime. If we are lucky to even have the smallest glimpse of this special being it must be grabbed and whatever message is conveyed to be responded to without delay. To those who are called by the Father it is written that He will over time reveal his special Son so we can learn about the way we need to love and serve God and one another. What I am really speaking about in this section is the day of visitation, a special day where it is decided if you are suitable to inherit eternal life.

History is filled with famous conversions of social dignitaries who having undergone years of rejecting Christ and his message then all of a sudden they 'see the light' and are converted. Their standing in society is still unchanged they still maintain their economic and social reputation in the public eye and glory not in God but in themselves. These types of 'false' followers have been the leaders and creators of many false and man made religions, responsible for the ongoing deception of poor lost souls, tired from the rigours of sin, who dream and hope for a better future.

I am sure that many men and women on this earth, having missed the 'today' of their salvation, years later subconsciously feel within themselves that something is missing in their lives and eventually realise that a life of atheism is a life without hope and start to manufacture their own conversion. Sadly this conversion is false and is maintained not by faith or by the prodding of God, but by their own sickly flesh and ambition.

Those of us who have realised the 'today' of salvation enjoy the abundance of spiritual power and help; having as a foundation true repentance and humble conversion away from an old life given up as an eternal sacrifice and laid at the feet of the Father and his holy throne.

In the New Testament, particularly in the writings of Paul, we read of a constant battle with false apostles and leaders who appear to rise up even within the gatherings of believers. They deceive and misguide and sadly, it appears, are an ongoing problem and burden to the Church of God.

There are four recognised books which describe Jesus' ministry on earth but it is the book of John which is an eye witness account and clearly the most reliable book of testaments. On the last night before Jesus was arrested in John's account the highlight and focus of the night was not on the dinner they had together but with Jesus formally washing the feet of all his disciples including Judas. The disciples are instructed to also wash each others feet from this demonstration. As a consequence of misguided and false teachers that followed after his death the focus of the last night of Jesus was shifted away from the extremely humbling foot washing ceremony to the more prideful dinner table.

Jesus was aware of man's fascination and obsession with food. Many times he tried to shift the focus of people way from worrying about material things including food and focussing more on seeking out our spiritual Father and his will. It was the disciples that were worried about feeding the masses that followed after them. It was also Mary, Jesus' mother, who was worried and influenced Jesus to change the water into wine not him. The focus of Jesus was never for us to be over-concerned about eating and drinking but to shift away and be just as concerned about making provision for God in our lives.

John the Baptist was said by Jesus to be in fact Elijah reincarnated. It may be strange to understand but when you go and look at the physical description of both men they were exactly the same. Both wore camels' skin with a leather belt for clothing and ate honey and locusts for food. According to Jesus John the Baptist was the greatest man to born of a woman. If we can use this man as an example of how we are to live, it can plainly be seen, 'the Baptist' was a man who was not obsessed with food or clothing. He was totally preoccupied with preaching the word of God and his continuing spiritual fellowship with the heavenly father. There is no doubt that Jesus did not expect us to pursue such a rigorous standard of self denial; but rather a moderation of all food intake with an increased emphasis on prayer and obedience to Gods words.

Paul who came to prominence after John [the Apostle], but still a formidable witness, writes about the Last Supper and suggested that as often as we eat and drink we are to remember how Jesus gave his own blood and body as a living and enduring sacrifice for us and all the world (I Cor. 11:24-26). In that reference it was never meant that we are to have a special ceremony where we invoke a special power to change the evening meal into some super drink and food. If this was the case then John would have mentioned this in his account but he gave it no importance rather focussing more on the foot washing ceremony.

The true dinner table is the one which involves eating together, in a spiritual sense, as revealed in a most wonderful passage written by John:

> Behold I stand at the door and knock. If anyone hears my voice and opens the door I will come into him and dine with him, and he with me. (Rev. 3:20)

I bring this point up only to highlight how far 'false teachers' have guided the supposed Christian world. Any 'real' Christian follower who is enjoying true spiritual help and power from above can only laugh at the futile and powerless ceremony of turning a meal into Jesus' body and blood. How did such a false teaching come into being? Through false teachers and in the minds of men clouded by their own sins without the faith or courage to live an honest life before God and men. Lost men and woman trying to justify and explain away their own original rejection of Jesus, rejecting the simplicity of his message about truth, love and justice.

15

The Unseen Church

Well here I am finally touching on what is an extremely clouded area and one which is continually ignored by even the most saintly scholars of this current world and of times past. The 'unseen church' as such is an interesting title yet brings with it such a ring of truth it makes it very difficult to by-pass as nothing.

Why is it ignored? Because what is unseen cannot bring money and what is unseen can only be seen with the eyes of faith. What was the main purpose of Jesus' work here on earth? Was it not to pull down the temple made with human hands and in three days build a new one, uncorrupted, pure and holy? When Jesus was in his trial witnesses came against him testifying that he was heard to have said that he would destroy the temple and rebuild it in three days. This was one of the main condemning testimonies against Jesus for which he was to actually die.

If we are to believe Jesus, and I do, then his main ministry and work on earth was to destroy the church and temple as it was known at that time. We know that Jesus never attacked the temple or church with a sledge hammer; but what he did do was attack verbally the formal religious structure and dignitaries of the day continually showing them to be hypocrites and without any connection with the real God in heaven. Rather Jesus quite plainly exposed them calling them children of the devil (John 8:44) and 'broods of vipers' (Matt.12:34).

I assume the actual destroying process of the temple structure was his three year ministry of continually going against the established system of the day. It does become a little confusing when Jesus also made use of the synagogue to preach, even presenting the declaration of his coming as prophesised by the prophet Isaiah. Yet his time allowed in these man-made places of worship was very quickly restricted by the Jews once they realised Jesus was using their own synagogues to ridicule and expose their lies and the empty religious rituals of the day.

It was also interesting that early in the ministry of Jesus he directly told the Samaritan woman at the well that 'the hour is coming when you will neither on this mountain, nor in Jerusalem, worship the Father' (John 4:23). From the very beginning he was directing people away from man-made structures and places of worship and attempted to redirect them to the new way of worshiping in 'the spirit and in truth' (John 4:24).

He gathered regularly with his disciples at the Mount of Olives and spent most of his time praying in private places often away from the people. If the local church or temple had any power at all then Jesus would have gone there to pray but he never did once. Even in choosing his disciples he chose a government tax collector before any person associated with the temple or local synagogue. His first disciples were originally disciples of John the Baptist. Judas could have also been a follower of 'the Baptist' moving on to following 'the crowd' so to speak.

So what have the religious buildings and self-proclaimed churches of Christ got to do with Jesus today? Well the answer is extremely simple as the message of Jesus himself: Nothing. They have absolutely nothing to do with Jesus if they are made with human hands. 'There shall not be left here one stone upon another that shall not be thrown down' (Matt. 24:2; Mark 13:2; Luke 21:6). Jesus clear intention in his mission was to remove the power and mystique of idolatrous church buildings and redirect people's energy into honest living and prayer to our 'unseen' God.

'For where two or three are gathered together in my name, there am I in the midst of them' (Matt.18:20). This is a unifying statement and a clear commitment by Jesus offering himself as an eternal and ongoing presence, which he is. This presence is much more than a man-made building constructed of stones and wood. Its covering is a personal spiritual presence, pure, clean and unpolluted by man. People coming together can be ministered to individually by Jesus and the Holy Spirit.

Man in his rebellion just cannot let go of a church made with bricks and mortar. Even to this very day they are being built, offering false hope and a powerless personal ministry. I could be attacked right here vehemently by faithful church-goers who for many years continue to congregate in the name of Jesus and who would claim that Jesus was in fact present at their meetings.

I dare say Jesus can be anywhere even in a pub; but the problem is man-made church is providing its own form of ministering to the people with prescribed rituals. "Oh our church is different" you may say; but all man-made churches are exactly the same but just in a different formulation. All have a pastor or leader who conducts the gathering and then there are the man-made rituals of the so-called 'service'. There is one religion which possibly could be excused from these harsh criticisms' of mine. These are the Quaker gatherings.

What really becomes annoying is when you see the latest trend in churches to call the local Church a 'place of worship'. This is complete heresy and wrong and far away from the true meaning of what church is meant to be since the coming of Jesus. We are to worship God '…in Spirit and in truth' (John 4:24). The spirit means privately and under the governance of the Holy Spirit; and in truth means to live a truthful and honest life before God and man. The truth is Jesus came to destroy man-made churches and if you are attending a man-made church then you are not living in truth. Ritual religion is not gathering together in the name of Jesus because it is not 'in truth'. You can scream and argue all day and all night but the God's family will have nothing to do with you as they all exist in total truth. In them is 'no lie' not a speck, not even the smallest microscopic blemish. God doesn't need some man-made bridge to be built up to him as any such thing will be thrown down. History has shown this anyway over and over again.

What we are commanded by God himself who was heard speaking from heaven is to 'hear him' (Matt.17:5). Hearing means to listen and to put into practice what Jesus told us to do. The Bible is filled with His words and we also have the truth now written on our hearts so in a way we have the bible written for us so there can be no mistake. Ignorance is a serious problem and even worse is allowing one's self to be ignorant.

Jesus was frustrated many times with the people. On one occasion he specifically stated that we are not to pray to the Father in ritual babblings but to make a personal type prayer to God as a child would speak to a father. But again man, as if on purpose, turns even Jesus' humble pleadings of the 'Our Father' prayer into a ritual prayer which is said over and over as if to invoke some magical power from heaven.

In all these things God has nothing to do with, he is just not interested. Rather he calls 'Come out of her, my people, lest you share in her sins' (Rev.18:4), is quoted referring to the mother of harlots, Babylon. Babylon literally means 'confusion' and for those still attending man-made churches you are still in serious confusion over what Jesus' whole mission and purpose is about. Confusion indeed gives birth to harlotry because in confusion the role of both men and women is lost and unknown.

One of the main reasons why we have so many churches in our society today is because the secular world in its blindness and ignorance has made provision for an organisation such as this to exist. These religious institutions operate as a type of 'exclusive' company with the added benefits of fantastic enterprising opportunities and tax concessions. Poor families without these same benefits are slowly syphoned dry with the increasing burden of taxes and extremely limited enterprising opportunity. Just as levels of Government grow year by year because of the biased flow of income and opportunity so also do man-made churches expand and grow even without a congregation present.

It doesn't suit the secular world to have an 'unseen' Church because this cannot be controlled or monitored. Rather it requires faith which 'earthly' eyes simply do not have.

'Except a man is born again, he cannot see the kingdom of God' (John 3:3), means quite simply changed from Adams seed into Jesus' and to have our eyes miraculously changed into the same eyes of our new father in Jesus, so to speak.

In secular society it is actually illegal to have a gathering of people for religious purposes without it being registered giving rise to regulatory control of gatherings. This is totally against the teachings of the New Testament. Therefore again a dilemma exists where to be a real [literal] Bible Christian wanting to gather with fellow believers without a permit is a secular crime in most western countries today. To not yield to the imposing laws of the land means you are a criminal and could spend time in prison contemplating the error of your ways.

History has shown us many examples of the shifting position of 'The Church' and secular society but I argue that no human being, society or group of people can quantity who are the chosen from the earth and the 'true' Church and people of God.

We read in the New Testament that the new Church has gates which Hell cannot prevail against and that it is enduring for ever more. History again has shown us thousands of man-made churches destroyed with its gates and walls easily breached even blown up. Jesus renamed the Apostle Simon— Peter 'Cephas' which means literally 'a Stone'. It's interesting because Peter later sets the standard on spiritual stones and accurately describes what the 'real' Church is. In his first epistle he explains that Jesus is the rejected key stone and 'You also, as living stones, are being built up a spiritual house' (I Pet. 2:5). We as 'living stones' are drawn together and taking our spiritual place side by side, stone next to stone together into a wonderful 'unseen' temple, serving and worshiping the living God day and night with our lives now and for all eternity.

Those of us who are living inside and are already part of this wonderful spiritual temple have no confusion as to who we are being drawn to. We are sharing in his sonship and also brotherhood, part of a holy priesthood, of the order of Melchizedek. As such we are expected to live as types of priests in total humility, diligence and continual prayer.

Having man-made counterfeit churches around us today is clearly an insult to the wonderful work of God and also the Son who continues to build up this 'unseen' spiritual building not made by human hands but his own. All man-made Churches around the world are painstakingly trying to replicate this magnificent spiritual building and priestly structures but they are old and dead as the altars of sacrifice that people of God once made burned offerings upon.

These man made churches of today even have the audacity to preach and enforce the old Mosaic law of tithing ten percent of wages; in turn draining poor families who are struggling to provide shelter and put food on their tables. Prior to Jesus priests at the temples laboriously performed vital services to the people which were essential for sanctification and cleansing. Jesus is now the high priest and is fulfilling these requirements for his people in an unseen temple away from human touch. Therefore current churches are fraudulently drawing funds from the people and will have to surely answer to God for this most cruel and deceptive lie.

In the beginning when there were no man-made structures or religious edifices there was a garden. It is also interesting to note that Jesus spent his last moments on earth not in a church or temple praying but in a garden. The problem with a garden it is not grandiose enough for the world. But be assured there is far more spiritual power drawn from a humble garden than one-hundred man made temples joined together.

I want to extend a little more on the 'unseen Church' and consider more intimately the enduring work of Christ. Lets us kneel, pray and give thanks to God 'who art' in heaven who has given us such a gracious gift to help us who struggle against our human condition and our real enemy ourselves and sin.

It is almost sacrilegious to use the name of Jesus as a name when he is so much more than just a name above all names. Being an actual Son is not a small thing when it comes to being the only Son of the highest entity in the universe and beyond. To imagine or visualise such a being with all his true power and glory sitting at the right hand of His Father is almost impossible because he is too great.

There have been a number of occasions where Christ appeared, once to Saul as a great light, and to John [Apostle] on the Island of Patmos with the countenance of the sun shining in its full strength. Anyone that comes from a hot and dry country can tell you that the Sun in its full strength is extremely powerful, far beyond even that of atomic power.

I have no need to sensationalise the Son of God or to build Him up in anyway. Whatever our feeble minds could ever conjure up would never come close to describing the brilliance of his greatness.

Yet with all this glory and greatness there is a very serious and enduring work which Christ continues to perform as I touched on earlier; that is the role of high priest. Jesus was always the high priest of the order of Melchizedek, the same priest that appeared to Abraham after his victory and the same priest 'who is seated at the right hand of the throne…a minister of the sanctuary and true tabernacle [building] which the Lord erected, and not man' (Heb. 8:2). The book of Hebrews reveals the true nature of Jesus as High priest and his direct [continued] association with the earth. It also describes the importance of a call of faith towards our high priest who we are trusting with our souls.

There is a saying that unless a person has a sore back they can never know or realise the pain of having back pain. Nobody really knows what Jesus as a high priest is doing from day-to-day and the struggles he endures at the right hand of the Father fulfilling all the necessary ceremonies and requirements. We have of course the earthly priests as an example which [also written] are but a shadow of the heavenly. There is mention that Jesus is a type of advocate pleading for those redeemed of the earth which brings to mind an image of an angry Judge requiring appeasing to minimise sentence.

The more bits and pieces we gather about Jesus and his enduring work the more humble one becomes. Silent, contemplative and regularly giving thanks when considering one's own salvation which is held in the fragile hands of all but one man.

16

The Memorial

It's funny as I could say every person that came across Jesus
wanted something from him. His enemies looked for fault and
weakness and opportunities to destroy and kill. His disciples
followed him as he was a teacher and could lead them to eternal
life. They even squabbled about who would be greatest even
wanting thrones and obvious power and glory for themselves.
The masses saw him as a liberator, a king who would liberate
them from the Romans and restore Israel to its former glory.
When Jesus' great healing powers were revealed people very
quickly began to seek after miracles, healings and even the
raising of their dead.

Then there was this one woman who did not seek anything at
all. She anointed Jesus' head with expensive oil which even
drew rebuke from his own disciples. Jesus said that wherever
the gospel of Jesus was preached that this woman would be
lifted up as an example and she indeed should be. This woman
in Simon the leper's house who anointed Jesus' head knew very
well that Jesus was about to endure something that no man or
woman has ever endured before. He was a most precious
person that is why she used expensive oil.

Jesus spoken openly about his departure while disciples often
squabbled about who was the greatest. Previously Peter had
also joined with Satan mocking his prophetic words. But this
humble woman was aware of the situation and in silence
anointed him with this most precious oil, which correctly should

have been. It's funny how immediately after this special moment of recognition by this lowly woman that Judas one of the elite twelve initiated 'the betrayal'.

I use the word betrayal in a plural sense as why were not the disciples anointing him and banding together preparing them selves even to die with him? Peter towards the end was the boldest but he was also found out to be one of the most cowardly and weakest. What of the other disciples? It is written that all 'forsook him' there was not one that stood with Jesus because to do so would of course meant to be caught up in 'the capture' and ultimately to die.

Yes John was recorded as being present at the death even following from a distance but was clearly lukewarm enough not to be caught up with the excitement of the moment. He in the end was left comforting Jesus' emotionally tortured [assumed] mother who was faced with watching the eldest child, who once lived for a time within her own womb, crucified.

I would rather call myself a coward ten times over than insult John or even dare call him anything other than a normal human maybe even the best example of human after the beheaded Baptist. Jesus plainly and openly at the end said that every disciple will be scattered 'each to his own'(John 16:32), in fact the point was already reached as Jesus was moving closer to 'his call' the disciples were detaching themselves further from him accusing him of speaking too figuratively.

Judas had already gone to get his detachment of officers for 'the arrest'. As recorded in the gospel of John there seemed to be a type of tension (chapter sixteen) where Jesus was painstakingly trying to explain what He was all about and what was about to happen. Jesus after laborious dialogue stated 'Do you now believe?' (John 16:31), implying that here at the end, after all he had been through with them, that only now they were starting to believe. Of course this is all silly for him to have to explain himself so much to the disciples who clearly were not one-hundred percent with him or even understanding him.

Human beings in their natural state do not have the qualities to do what is right either in the presence of the living God [Jesus] or especially in his absence. The disciples were the closest to Jesus yet it was proved at the end that it really made no difference. The woman who anointed his head, wasn't even with Jesus, yet was there at his departure somehow sensing within his real importance to our world.

What this woman was highlighting in a sense was the change-over point of a new age or time on the earth. It is clear in the writings especially of Peter that after Jesus was resurrected and ascended that he (Peter) matured and developed into a clear and sober follower of Jesus, well able to recognise and instruct with things pertaining to the kingdom. Jesus hinted to the ignorant disciples that it was necessary for the world for Him to leave the earth.

A memorial can be an important milestone but it is only something which marks a point reached in the past. What is more important I think is not so much the past but what wonderful things that can now happen now in the future?

17

The Quiet Achiever

*Oh Earth how beautiful, like a jewel in the sky of peace,
how long I've cried! How long I've called! But you were
never to know the deep love I had for you from the
moment you were born.*

The focus or imagery of the world has always been on the
Father and his Son. While people contemplate this interesting
phenomenon they readily struggle, actual fail, to conceptualise
the third part of God whom I call the quiet achiever, the Holy
Spirit of God. Probably the most neglected and misunderstood
part of Christ's mission and the fundamental life giver firstly to
Jesus then to a people once forsaken and lost.

We have the Father who about whom, Jesus said, 'You have
not heard his voice, nor seen his form' (John 5:37) and we can
never know unless he is revealed to us with the help of the Son.
Then no one can know the Son without being drawn to and
manifested by the Father. This is a very difficult situation and
clearly Jesus hinted to the answer with his analogy with the wind.
'The wind blows where it wishes' (John 3:8): being of course the
Holy Spirit who Jesus told his disciples is another helper to
come.

As is often referred to in all the scriptures the Holy Spirit is both He and She, a special spirit which is why she is called Holy. Largely unseen and not known by the world she possesses so many special things that description very quickly carries beyond the confines of human conceptual understanding.

There is one occasion that the Holy Spirit as a person is manifested for a moment but I am sure there are many other occasions hidden within the scriptures. The time I refer to is at the baptism of Christ in Luke's account.

It is written that while Jesus was baptised he prayed '...the heaven was opened and the Holy Spirit descended in bodily form like a dove upon him' (Luke 3:22). The words 'bodily form' I am sure implies a human like image or manifestation which easily could be male or even female. Only eye witnesses including Jesus himself could provide a more detailed description of that event.

The world in its fleshly ignorance always likes to attach idol imagery to any divinity attributing the simplistic dove which is in actuality very wrong as I am sure it is much more than that. The dove refers to the way the Holy Spirit descended, being ever so gentle. It is of course possible that the humanoid form of the Holy Spirit is very much birdlike but gigantic and most certainly possesses the sensitivity of a rare bird being of course 'one of a kind'. One could go even further to say that this birdlike being was in fact the ancient mythical phoenix come back to the earth.

This ancient bird was said to have lived for 500 years then build a nest and burn itself with fire than arise again for another five-hundred years and so on it lives forever more. In the book of Job (29:18) there is a reference to a nest and 'multiply my days as sand [chol] (old king James version)' which has three translation meanings; phoenix, palm tree, or sand. It is also interesting at the time of Pentecost when the Holy Spirit was first sent to the apostles by Jesus from the 'other' world there was a rushing mighty wind then tongues of fire appeared and rested upon their heads (Acts 2:2-3). The mythical bird has always been associated with fire and resurrection as it 'rises out of the ashes' to live another 500 years as the story goes.

The heavens being opened implied that the Holy Spirit [the Phoenix] was not already on the earth and had been locked away in heaven, so to speak, until the time had come that a human being had fulfilled all that was needed to fulfil being the law and requirements of the Father to enable the natural release of this most precious being.

It was after this time that Jesus formally began his public miracles displaying fantastic powers, performing miracles and unusual feats such as walking on water and travelling 'in the power of the Spirit' (Luke 4:14) across hundreds of miles to Galilee in a short amount of time. John said at the end of his account that there was also many other things that Jesus did and if each account was written one by one not even all the books in the world could contain everything. It doesn't matter really. The fact remains that even one miracle of Jesus was fantastic enough to establish him as special and the most important person to this world.

The Old Testament mentions a spirit as such, 'thus says the spirit of the lord' but this spirit is rather a type of presence to assist in prophesying rather than the actual Holy Spirit as a separate and unique Godhead entity.

There is only one place in the Old Testament that I know that records the actual Holy Spirit speaking directly about her self and that is in chapter eight: verses 12 to 36. In all the Bible there doesn't exist a more precious untouched or unpolluted jewel. Here we learn so much about the personality of the Holy Spirit, what she likes and her role and place along side with God, even before the universe or earth was created:

> *Then I was beside him as a master craftsman; and I was daily His delight, rejoicing always before Him, Rejoicing in His inhabited World. And my delight was with the sons of men.* (Pro.8:30-31)

What's sad is that the whole verse is actually written in a type of past tense with the extended use of the word, 'was', and seems to fit with a progressive disconnection with the earth over time. This is in line with the growth or rise of sin upon the earth up until our current time. When the earth was created sin was not part of the Holy Spirit's construction plans and I am sure as far as sin is concerned she continues to exist and live in a world maybe even a universe away from this place.

Initially the Holy Spirit would have found delight in 'the son's men' but as they turned to sin this would have 'grieved' her away to cause her to be locked in heaven. If the Holy Spirit was not held there, then there would not have been such a dramatic re-opening ceremony at the baptism of Jesus 2000 years ago.

Sometimes when you look around at all of nature and the wonders of the earth there is type of loneliness or rather emptiness a sense that something is missing, a linkage of sorts to the universe and the real purpose to why we are all here. Our planet as beautiful as it is seems at times to be all alone at the end of a dark endless universe. Death itself has become like a fearful blanket appearing to be our only transition point between this world and the unknown. It was never meant to be like this, the rejoicing Holy Spirit of old would never allow such a fearful transition as thousands of human beings experience now and every day.

Jesus made special mention to his disciples that he had to leave and that he would send the Holy Spirit which he saw as a crucial missing presence and linkage to the earth. He spoke of the Holy Spirit being a guide to truth, to help convict the world of sin, a teacher, a comforter and personal companion that would help us not to feel so alone.

The Holy Spirit was already gone a long time ago and the earth was truly dying, diseased and wandering, lost in the wilderness. What did Jesus do to unblock or bring back the Holy Spirit to this earth? He never told us but it was something very special and I am sure part of Jesus' pleadings before the Father which He does day and night.

In this world which is often referred to as a 'mans world', the role of a woman is both clouded and in most parts of the world distorted. It is written actually that more women followed Jesus than men. It is openly accepted that Jesus was in fact the first real liberator of women putting his own life at risk intervening in a violent stoning of a woman found guilty of the act of adultery.

Women have a very difficult struggle in this world, far more than any man's. Firstly she is generally physically weaker than men and is in a continual struggle to fight for rights which men in ways are born possessing. If a woman escapes the stereotype of a sex object or working slave she is then thrust into a heavily competitive world largely controlled by men. The majority of women of the world today are still regarded as second class citizens, especially in the Middle East and Asia.

In the flesh Paul also set a difficult standard for men, women and children alike to live under a continual cloud and line of submission with Christ at the head; But the reality and truth as established by John (Apostle) is that men and women are in fact equal heirs serving together side by side as high priests in a part of a holy 'unseen' temple with Jesus.

I want to uncover here a wonderful truth and mystery in total clarity, an intended relationship and calling that we are to have with the Holy Spirit.

In chapter seven of Proverbs we are introduced to the harlot, the immoral woman, '…the seductress who flatters with her words (Prov.7:5). She stands at every street corner 'lurking'. She is married and her husband is not at home and will come at a set time. 'With her enticing speech she caused him to yield…He did not know it would cost his life' (Prov. 7:21-23) It goes on to say that: 'Her house is the way to hell, descending to the chambers of death' (Prov.7:27).

Immediately after this in chapter eight the Holy Spirit introduces herself also as a woman who '…cries out by the gates, at the entry of the city' (Prov.8:3), making herself available to all men from on top of a high hill calling out: 'To you, O Men, I call, and my voice is to the sons of men' (Prov.8:4).This is followed with all the wonderful promises and beautiful revelations that can be obtain to all that go her way.

The Holy Spirit deliberately presents herself contrastingly and purposely against the immoral woman as if they are set at poles apart. In the next chapter (nine) it is declared that 'She [Holy Spirit] has sent out her maidens' (Prov.9:3), here we learn that the woman's real place is to be prepared [first] and then 'sent out' to love men guided by the Holy Spirit and not by their own devises or plans.

In a world where the woman's role seems very confusing, and at times lost, there is the Holy Spirit offering herself as the preparer and lover of men which is her characteristic trade mark. I don't believe there is any excuse or room to move for a woman who has chosen the immoral path and for the man which followers after her 'But he does not know that the dead are there, that her guests are in the depths of hell' (Prov. 9:18).

This world today just glories in this immorality, women and men, younger and younger fall into this trap together with the cycle of destruction and despair. The line truly needs to be drawn and people must take a stand against this slippery path. As discussed in an earlier chapter Hell is not a joke and the Hell which has already risen upon this earth does not care about whom it gobbles up or contains.

For the woman she must embrace the Holy Spirit and her ways and learn how to serve and love her fellow man with kindness with a pure and clean heart. For the man he must run from the immoral woman and not desire her plastic images joining in her rebellion against her husband, her family and Holy Spirit who has called her from her youth.

18

True Repentance and Love

One of the reasons why I have decided to touch on this topic at the end of this book is because repentance and love are probably the two most important areas seriously misconstrued and misunderstood. I covered repentance in chapter one when I wrote about reconciliation with God. What is broken remains broken until it is repaired or restored. Yet true repentance is fundamental to any earthly hope of restoration between us and our God 'who art' in heaven.

Again I don't want to get into any debates about believing or not believing in God as an 'ever present' interactive spirit; but ultimately I want the reader to understand that without true repentance there cannot be any real relationship of any substance between us and our maker but only the expectation of 'fearful expectation of judgement' (Heb.10:27).

What also makes this subject interesting is that repentance is actually a gift under the umbrella of grace from the Father to help us work our way back to peaceful fellowship with him. Where an 'axe is laid to the root of the trees' (Matt. 3:10), we start our journey to him from a very difficult position. As previously discussed the natural unrenewed man is being convicted of sin by the Holy Spirit. Day and night the quiet achiever works gently showing us our need for help that we are sinners daily hurting our creator, people around us and creation itself.

The spirit searches deep within the heart speaking to us, convicting, telling us we have gone astray and need to return to our ever so loving creator. Some harden their hearts rejecting the loving convictions running deeper and deeper into sin and corruption. Eventually a point is reached which is determined by the Father and the conviction is removed and replaced with Judgment. Judgment means it is all over; no right of appeal. The decision is made to hand that person to his heart's desire and the consequences of sin takes full effect, which is of course death.

There is again an exemption to this final judgment which is described in John's book of Revelation. At the final judgment of the world Hell will be raised up and its occupants will again face a form of final judgment and those found in the 'Lamb's book of life' (Rev. 21:27) will be liberated to everlasting life and the rest will be finally destroyed in a sea of sulphur along with Satan and the fallen angels. To some especially those before 'the flood' Hell is like a very long gaol sentence alone in a cell contemplating the extremity of the distance reached between themselves and those in heaven who 'shall go forth and look upon the corpses of men' who have offended God as is written in the last verse of Isaiah.

To those who respond to the Spirit's conviction it is a different story. Some people may be limited in their responses to God and attempt to adjust their life to restrict harm they 'do to others' and in so doing try to live an honest life and at times speak to the Father as a type of distant friend or companion. Yet the conviction will remain with them all of their lives but in a continual state of rebellion and ignorance they never reach a point of reconciliation. Their fate is a type of gamble and God will himself decide who goes where and what if any punishments will be inflicted.

Those who eventually yield to the conviction of wrong and sincerely repent before the host of heaven have an opportunity to walk on a path to eternal life. John the Baptist clearly established repentance as a prerequisite to Salvation further explaining that 'fruits of repentance' (Matt. 3:8) go hand in hand with real repentance.

It is quite simple really; the same God who made eyes for us to see can also see genuine shame and one's struggle to restore what has been stolen or trespasses done to other human beings. It isn't so much what you have done to God, rather what harm you have done to fellow human beings that need restoring and reconciling first. You can cry and pray a thousand prayers but 'first be reconciled to your brother, and then come and offer your gift' (Matt. 5:24). Because if you can't reconcile with people you can see and harmed then how can you reconcile with a God you cannot see?

The truth is if you genuinely are ashamed of something you will stop doing it with all the human power available to you. Jesus even stated that if something causes you to sin 'cut it off'

(Matt.5:30). We know very well what cause us to sin. What friends we hang around, places we visit, including inappropriate web sites.

John the Baptist was in a way the pinnacle of the human race. There is a mystery about how he really became 'the Baptist'. Yet his whole being and purpose was devoted to the word 'repent'. This call was not in the synagogues of cities or the towns but in the wilderness. People who are called to be with God must make the journey alone away from the world to the very fringe of society. For some the journey is forced upon them because of the rigors of life. To others they become disillusioned with the status quo and seek a new way and home wondering the extremities of earth.

In the end it has to be love which drives any man or woman to the wilderness in search of a God 'out there' that may help and care for our weary souls. If there is no love then there really isn't anything worth striving for. What we do know is that 'God is Love' (1Joh.4:8). If God is love then it is clear that we can only truly know love if we find God. If love isn't our motivation then our journey is indeed in vain and we would very quickly return back to the safety of the loveless city.

Why really does God bother with us? Having cast us away so many times, lowered us below even the lowest, struck us with his own hand, it must be that he truly does love us if he has put so much effort into 'raising up' Prophets to help and guide us time after time. He must really care for us as he is often given last place in our lives and tirelessly waits for us to acknowledge his constant love even in a small way. He must really care about us if he has indeed given as is written 'his only begotten son' (John 3:16). Nobody can love us like our creator can, no human being or created thing, nothing. He made and designed us, he knows every curve, every shape, everything we are and are to become. It is in allowing ourselves to be loved by God that we ourselves learn about love and can in turn love others.

God does love you and can prove His love to all human beings if they would hear His call to them to draw closer to him. He has given all He could give to enable a path for us to find Him again after it was long lost and forgotten. The rest is really up to us to leave all the fleshly things we cling to and take small steps towards Him. And you will find him there waiting for you as a loving father waiting for a much beloved child to return to him after a long journey far far away.

Christ is only a dilemma to those who don't want to know God and real sincere love will always bridge any gap of ignorance or uncertainty. The call to God is really a call to love and 'to be loved'. For those who do not venture to the wilderness and find 'the waters' they will remain forever dry and lifeless, always bound in ignorance and left wondering what could have been. But for those few who stumble across the 'hidden treasure in the field' (Matt. 13:44), they will find enduring peace and rest to their weary souls forever.

Final Message

The Christ dilemma I believe is the same dilemma that Adam and Eve had to face in the beginning and what Lucifer also may have faced before going on to sabotage God's deeply loved creation; us. The dilemma has always been to either accept the living word that 'dwelt among us' (John 1:14) or to question and reject his presence and every word spoken as worthless or wrong.

This book was written in the hope that I may encourage other pilgrims on the journey of truth. I am not talking about those who say a church bred prayer, condition themselves into believing they are followers of the living God. Then in a sickly manner continue in their delusion secretly continuing old ways. Lying, drinking, cheating, stealing, lusting, oppressing the weak; continuing to serve the idol of themselves and not allowing the spirit to enter in and God to sit on the throne of their life.

I join with those few individuals whom have, in a holy and sacred time, sorrowfully emptied themselves before the Godhead family. Then in a moment of grace received concession for their shameful ways and started on the road of reconciliation. Not as Peter puts it, 'as a dog returning to its own vomit' (II Pet. 2:22), but as a 'once prisoner', freed, appreciative of every second of freedom from the jail of his sinful flesh.

In a way here in this book, I embrace you as family. I love you and look forward to sharing together the new world Jesus is now preparing as promised. A place where there will be no more sickness, death, or tears and disappointment but rather real joy and laughter, all bad things associated with sin and evil will be cast far away.

When one surrenders to the family of God no one expects to have the hard life and struggles that comes with the journey. They enter a new world which is very hard to understand, especially the many negative forces which seemingly come against you. Many of Jesus' words are beyond human understanding, He spoke as giving one's life for the sake of truth as nothing and what was done to him were in fact 'times of green'. What will happen to those warriors and pilgrims of truth of today when the times are dry? So many questions and truths to consider, this is when it becomes easier to just trust and follow the words and directions of a guide. There is only one 'good shepherd,' and He Himself has sent us the Holy Spirit whom has a presence all of her own; delivering us who struggle, loving, guiding, teaching and rendering peace even in the face of torture and threat of death.

In Gods sight those of us who are in Christ are sinless free to approach the very altar and for him to bless us with his many delights. Of course we are all aware of our potential sinfulness of the old beast that lingers underneath; but our sinning has ceased or in the process of ceasing.

Did this guy say, ceasing from sin? Yes I did say that and so did Jesus as this was the sole purpose of his coming to this planet, to put a stop finally to sin.

Oh of course the opposition doesn't like me talking about such things. The fallen angel would say even now: "I stopped this type of nonsense long time ago, Jesus didn't really tell that man he cured from his sickness to 'sin no more lest a worse thing come upon you'. Jesus didn't really tell the woman who was being stoned for adultery to 'sin no more'."

This book is not about Lucifer, but about truth. The real truth is accepting that we human beings in our fallen condition are barely worthy or able to manage correctly the delicate and precious words associated with Christ. This is why Jesus clearly associated the administration of truth to be conducted by the workings of the Holy Spirit, and let it be so.

The words of this book are certainly not supportive of any current ideals and practices of government which assumes an ambient persona of truth. Rather what is written herein is part of a continuing protest against lies and injustices. I formally and proudly join together with the honourable men and women of today and times past who were struck down in violence while proclaiming truth. How can it be another is writing and declaring such things? Well Jesus is still alive although currently occupied with his continual pleadings before the Father He is expecting us to awake from our drugged slumber and help Him in his work of spreading a fire upon the earth which will be a true offering an acceptable and sweet smelling aroma to our God and master when he soon returns.

It was never God's intention for the human race to be destroyed along with Lucifer but we will suffer exactly the same fate if we do not work hard to reconcile with God even from our fallen condition.

Of course if you are unsure of where you stand before God and feel this thinking is all a bit weird, well maybe this book is not one that you should be reading. You could be saying to yourself even now "this author is bit lost and in need of some serious therapy." Or as you read the words of the chapters you feel very tired as if yours eyes are sleepy. Well? Go and have a nice long sleep. May the God of your choice be with you in your sweet dreams.

You can easily join with the disciples on the Mount of Olives as they slept when Jesus was praying at his last moments of freedom upon the earth. Sleep as Jesus struggled in anguish having to face the full might of Satan on his own in his weakened human condition; seeing ahead his betrayal, denial, physical torture and ultimate killing. Going on to bear all sins and sickness of all chosen peoples of the earth who just don't understand or really care. Sleep while others stand up uncomforted by luxuries of man-made churches and religion. Sleep as others fight the good fight. Enjoy your rest as 'others' are sent to the slaughter while spreading the gospel message with the gentle hand of peace.

About the Author

Ivan Joseph Markov born on 22nd of February1964 in Melbourne, Australia to Croatian and Hungarian immigrant parents, Joseph Markov and Ildiko Banhidi. At the age of four the family moved to the then Australian Territory of Papua New Guinea.

Joseph [his father], a Senior Engineer draftsman, was stationed initially on Bougainville Island. The family later moved to Port Moresby, the capital, where he began a number of business enterprises whilst employed at the Public Works Department.

Ivan, the eldest of four children, attended a number of International schools which were shared with other expatriate children mostly from Australia and New Zealand.

Violence erupted with independence of a new nation looming and in January 1975 the family moved to Brisbane on the east coast of Australia. It was here that he was to continued his primary and then secondary education at St Thomas Moore College, Sunnybank Hills.

He went on from there to attend the Queensland University of Technology where he completed three qualifications. His first being a Bachelor of Applied Science (Built Environment), awarded in 1986. With a mid-course transfer into a new course was later awarded a Bachelor of Architecture in 1989. With ten years of private and public practice, he became disillusioned with industry and moved into the field of eco-education. He later returned to studies at QUT in 2002; where he eventually went on to complete a Graduate Diploma in Education in 2006.

Some of his professional achievements include numerous individual and group design projects such as; to prepare and document a design submission for a national monument to commemorate the centenary of federation of 2001(invited by the State and then Premier of Queensland); Establishing and registering the Progress Party of Australia in 2002.

On a personal level becoming a father of four children, Sarah, Ruth, Noah and Samuel is regarded as his "greatest accomplishment and joy." Among other pursuits and achievements must go towards his singing/song writing, performing and recording. He is also an internationally recognised children and social activist, nature lover and keen horticulturalist.

www.ingramcontent.com/pod-product-compliance
Lightning Source LLC
Chambersburg PA
CBHW032101080426
42733CB00006B/370